Excel

Get the Results You Want!

Year 2 NAPLAN*-style Tests

Associate Professor James Athanasou with Angella Deftereos

PASCAL PRESS

© 2011 James Athanasou, Angella Deftereos and Pascal Press
New NAPLAN Test question formats added 2012
Reprinted 2014 (twice)
Conventions of Language questions updated 2018

Revised in 2020 for the NAPLAN Online tests

Reprinted 2020, 2021, 2022

ISBN 978 1 74125 409 9

Pascal Press
PO Box 250
Glebe NSW 2037
(02) 8585 4050
www.pascalpress.com.au

Publisher: Vivienne Joannou
Project editor: Mark Dixon
Edited by Rosemary Peers
Proofread and answers checked by Peter Little and Dale Little
Cover and page design by DiZign Pty Ltd
Typeset by DiZign Pty Ltd, Kim Webber and Grizzly Graphics (Leanne Richters)
Printed by Vivar Printing/Green Giant Press

CONTENTS

Welcome to the *Excel Year 2 NAPLAN*-style Tests*. This book has been specifically written to help parents and teachers of Year 2 students in their preparation for the Year 3 NAPLAN Tests. It is also helpful as general revision for Year 2.

Please note that there are no Year 2 NAPLAN Tests. There are only Year 3 and Year 5 NAPLAN Tests in primary school.

This book was first published in 2011 and was revised for NAPLAN changes several times. It has been widely used and many thousands of copies have been published throughout the years. In this edition the content has been reorganised for the new online version of the NAPLAN Tests.

The aim of this brief introduction is to provide parents, guardians and teachers with some background to NAPLAN.

The book is a collaboration by a specialist in educational testing and an experienced NAPLAN marker. Both are trained teachers.

It is designed for use by parents who want to help their son or daughter, and by teachers who wish to prepare their class for the NAPLAN Tests. Some parents also use these books for general revision or when tutoring their son or daughter.

We hope that you will find this guide easy to use. In the following sections we will try to answer some frequently asked questions about the tests.

Associate Professor James Athanasou, LittB, MA, PhD, DipEd, MAPS

Angella Deftereos, BA, MTeach

What is different about this edition?

This is the latest and most thorough revision of the Year 2 book. It has been designed to accommodate the new online tests in an easy-to-use book format. The tests in this book contain excellent practice questions from very easy to very hard.

What is NAPLAN?

NAPLAN stands for *National Assessment Program—Literacy and Numeracy*. It is the largest educational testing program in Australia. It is conducted every year and the tests are taken by students in Year 3, Year 5, Year 7 and Year 9. All students in these year levels are expected to participate in the tests.

The tests cover Reading, Writing, Conventions of Language (Spelling, Grammar and Punctuation) and Numeracy. In other words, they cover what are known to many people as the basic skills of reading, writing and arithmetic.

What is the purpose of NAPLAN?

Although NAPLAN has been designed mainly to provide administrators and politicians with information about Australian schools and educational systems, it is also relevant for each pupil. It provides a public record of their educational achievement.

Increasingly it is among the most valuable series of tests students will undertake in their primary schooling and probably their first formal and public examination.

What is being assessed?

The content of NAPLAN is based on what is generally taught across Australia. So do not be surprised if NAPLAN does not match exactly what each child is learning in their class. Most schools should be teaching more than the basic levels.

NAPLAN covers only a specific range of skills. This is because literacy and numeracy are considered to be the basis of future learning in school. Of course we know that there are many other personal or social skills that are important in life.

We also realise that each child has their own special talents and aptitudes but at the same time governments also want to be able to assess their educational achievement in the fundamental skills. It is important to emphasise that there are many different kinds of literacy and numeracy, and that these tests cover only some aspects.

What is NAPLAN Online?

Until 2017 NAPLAN Tests were all paper tests. From 2022 all students will take NAPLAN Online, with the exception of the Year 3 Writing Test which will remain a paper test. Students will complete the tests on a computer or on a tablet. With NAPLAN paper tests, all students in each year level took exactly the same tests. In the NAPLAN Online tests this won't be the case; instead, every student will take a tailor-made test based on their ability.

In the NAPLAN Online tests a student is given specially selected questions that try to match their ability. This means that in theory a very bright student should not have to waste time answering very easy questions. Similarly, in theory, a student who is not so capable should not be given difficult questions that are far too hard for them.

Please visit the official ACARA site for a detailed explanation of the tailored test process used in NAPLAN Online and also for general information about the tests: https://nap.edu.au/online-assessment.

These tailor-made tests will mean broadly, therefore, that a student who is at a standard level of achievement will take a test that is mostly comprised of questions of a standard level; a student who is at an intermediate level of achievement will take a test that is mostly comprised of questions of an intermediate level; and a student who is at an advanced level of achievement will take a test that is mostly comprised of questions of an advanced level.

Do the tests in this book match those in NAPLAN Online?

The practice tests in this book build up gradually in length in order to increase the test-taking stamina of very young students. The final practice test in each of Reading, Conventions of Language and Numeracy is the same length as in NAPLAN Online. This book provides items across a wide range of difficulty.

Of course there is no way of predicting what actual questions will be asked but practice using these questions will help to familiarise a student with the content of the tests.

Naturally there will be some questions that can be presented on a computer that are harder to present in a book, but the content and skills will be similar.

Like in the NAPLAN Online tests, there are multiple-choice questions in this book but there are some differences. The spelling test is a good example. In the computer version the words are dictated by the computer. We cannot do this in a book but we have prepared a list of words for parents, guardians or teachers to dictate.

Are the questions in this book similar to those in NAPLAN Online?

Parents can have confidence that the questions in this book reflect the online NAPLAN. We believe that we have covered all the types of questions in a convenient book format.

On the whole it is our impression that some of the questions in this book will be much harder than those in NAPLAN. We have deliberately included some more challenging questions.

We have also made a special effort to cover as many different question formats as possible. For instance, spelling questions have been altered to be given orally to the student.

Naturally it is not possible to use the same processes as the online test, such as click and drag, but it is possible to use the same thinking processes.

The Check your skills pages after each test suggest the approximate level of difficulty of questions so you can see what levels of difficulty of questions a student is able to answer.

On the Check your skills pages, questions are divided into standard, intermediate or advanced. This will help you prepare for the standard, intermediate or advanced test that your child will sit. Please refer to page 31 to see an example of a checklist page from the book.

Please refer to the next page to see some examples of question types that are found in NAPLAN Online and how they compare to questions in this book. As you will see, the content tested is exactly the same but the questions are presented differently.

NAPLAN Online question types	Equivalent questions in Reading Tests in this book
Dropdown list Here is a picture of some money. Use the tab to answer the question. This money came from Australia. ↓ New Zealand. United Kingdom.	Here is a picture of some money. To answer this question colour in the circle with the correct answer. From which country did this money come? ○ Australia ○ New Zealand ○ United Kingdom
Identifying/sorting Click on the picture that shows binoculars.	Which picture shows binoculars? ○ ○ ○

NAPLAN Online question types	Equivalent questions in Numeracy Tests in this book
Online ruler Here is a piece of wood. Use the online ruler to measure it. About how long is this piece of wood? ☐ 40 cm ☐ 45 cm ☐ 50 cm ☐ 55 cm	Imagine a long piece of wood. This is measured by a tape or ruler. This tape is marked in centimetres About how long is this piece of wood? ○ 40 cm ○ 45 cm ○ 50 cm ○ 55 cm

NAPLAN Online question types	Equivalent questions in Conventions of Language Tests in this book
Drag and drop Drag the correct word to fill in the space. | is		are		am | Many people ▭ fishing.	Choose the correct word to fill each gap. Colour in only one circle for each answer. Many people ▭ fishing. is are am ○ ○ ○
Click Which words in the sentence should have a capital letter? 	the	australian	team	played
italy	in	the	final.		Three capital letters have been left out of this sentence. Which words should start with a capital letter? the australian team played italy in the final. ○ ○ ○ ○ ○ ○ ○ ○
Text entry Where do you _____? Click on the play button to listen to the missing word. ‖ ◁)) ──────● 0.08 / 0.09 Type the correct spelling of the word in the box. ▭	Ask your teacher or parent to read the spelling words for you. The words are listed on page 240. Write the spelling words on the lines below. ✏ **Test 6 spelling words** 26. _____ **Spelling words for Conventions of Language Test 6** 	Word	Example
26. live	Where do you live?	

As you can see there are differences between the processes involved in answering the questions in NAPLAN Online and this book but we think they are minimal.

Nevertheless we **strongly advise** that students should practise clicking and dragging until they are **familiar** with using a computer or tablet to answer questions.

What are the advantages of revising for the NAPLAN Online tests in book form?

There are many benefits to a child revising for the online test using books.

- One of the most important benefits is that writing on paper will help your child retain information. It can be a very effective way to memorise. High quality educational research shows that using a keyboard is not as good as note-taking for learning.

- Students will be able to prepare thoroughly for topic revision using books and then practise computer skills easily. They will only succeed with sound knowledge of topics; this requires study and focus. Students will not succeed in tests simply because they know how to answer questions digitally.

- Also, some students find it easier to concentrate when reading a page in a book than when reading on a screen.

- Furthermore it can be more convenient to use a book, especially when a child doesn't have ready access to a digital device.

- You can be confident that **Excel** books will help students acquire the topic knowledge they need, as we have over 30 years experience in helping students prepare for tests. All our writers are experienced educators.

How *Excel Test Zone* can help you practise online

We recommend you go to www.exceltestzone.com.au and register for practice in NAPLAN Online–style tests once you have completed this book. The reasons include:

- for optimal performance in the NAPLAN Online tests we strongly recommend students gain practice at completing online tests as well as completing revision in book form

- students should practise answering questions on a digital device to become confident in this process

- students will be able to practise tailored tests like those in NAPLAN Online as well as other types of tests

- students will also be able to gain valuable practice in onscreen skills such as dragging and dropping answers, using an online ruler to measure figures and using an online protractor to measure angles.

Remember that **Excel Test Zone** has been helping students prepare for NAPLAN since 2009; in fact we had NAPLAN online questions even before NAPLAN tests went online!

We also have updated our website along with our book range to ensure your preparation for NAPLAN Online is 100% up to date.

What do the tests indicate?

They are designed to be tests of educational achievement; they show what a person has learnt or can do.

They are not IQ tests. Probably boys and girls who do extremely well on these tests will be quite bright. It is possible, however, for some intelligent children to perform poorly because of disadvantage, language, illness or other factors.

Are there time limits?

Yes, there are time limits for each test. These are usually set so that 95% of pupils can complete the tests in the time allowed.

If more than one test is scheduled on a day then there should be a reasonable rest break of at least 20 minutes between tests. In some special cases pupils may be given some extra time and allowed to complete a response.

Who does the NAPLAN Tests?

The NAPLAN Testing Program is held for pupils in Year 3 each year. The tests are designed for all pupils.

Some schools may exempt pupils from the tests. These can include children in special English classes and those who have recently arrived from non–English speaking backgrounds or children with special needs.

Our advice to parents and guardians is that children should only undertake the tests if it is likely to be of benefit to them. It would be a pity if a pupil was not personally or emotionally ready to perform at their best and the results underestimated their ability. The results on this occasion might label them inaccurately and it would be recorded on their pupil record card. Some parents have insisted successfully that their child be exempt from testing.

Who developed these tests?

The tests were developed especially by ACARA. These are large-scale educational tests in which the questions are trialled extensively. Any unsuitable questions will be eliminated in these trials. They should produce results with high validity and reliability.

How can the results be used?

The results of the NAPLAN Tests offer an opportunity to help pupils at an early stage. The findings can be used as early indicators of any problem areas.

It would be a pity to miss this chance to help boys or girls at this stage in their schooling when it is relatively easy to address any issues. The findings can also be used as encouragement for pupils who are performing above the minimum standard.

It is important for parents and teachers to look closely at the student report. This indicates the areas of strength and weakness. The report can be a little complex to read at first but it contains quite a helpful summary of the skills assessed in Reading, Writing, Conventions of Language and Numeracy. Use this as a guide for any revision.

If NAPLAN indicates that there are problems, then repeated testing with other measures of educational achievement is strongly recommended. It is also relevant to compare the results of NAPLAN with general classroom performance.

Remember that all educational test results have limitations. Do not place too much faith in the results of a single assessment.

Does practice help?

There is no benefit in trying to teach to the test because the questions will vary from year to year. Nevertheless a general preparation for the content of NAPLAN Tests should be quite helpful. Some people say that practising such tests is not helpful but we do not agree.

Firstly practice will help to overcome unfamiliarity with test procedures. Secondly it will help pupils deal with specific types of questions. Test practice should help students perform to the best of their ability.

Use the tests in this book to practise test skills and also to diagnose some aspects of learning in Year 2. In saying this parents should make sure their child is interested in undertaking these practice tests. There is no benefit in compelling children to practise.

Sometimes it is easy to forget that they are still young children. We recommend that you sit with them or at least stay nearby while they are completing each test. Give them plenty of praise and encouragement for their efforts.

How are students graded?

One of the big advantages of NAPLAN is that it uses a single scale of achievement. This has 10 levels of achievement that are called bands. It will then be possible for you to see how much progress has been made by each pupil in literacy and numeracy from Year 3 to Year 9. Normally we would expect pupils to increase their level of achievement at each stage. In this book we have tried to grade the questions into levels for you.

Each year covers different bands. In Year 3 there are six achievement bands. Students who are in the lowest band (Band 1) are considered to be below the minimum standard. Students who are at Band 2 in Year 3 are performing at the national minimum standard. Students who are in Bands 3 to 6 are performing above the national minimum standard.

What results are provided to parents?

Parents receive comprehensive test results, as do teachers and schools. These enable interpretation of results at a personal and a group level.

The parent reports will show performance in broad skill bands. Some people will look only at the band reached on these tests but really it is more important to see what the student knows or can do.

The bands covering the middle 60% of the students have been shaded in a lighter colour in the report provided to parents. This is called the average range. But it is quite a large group. There is a huge difference between the pupils who are at the top and bottom of this average range. Averages tend to hide more than they reveal but it will be possible to see whether a pupil is performing above or below the expected range of performance.

Each band will list the child's skills in the area of literacy and numeracy. The results are not straightforward to interpret and some assistance may be required. The bands are not a percentage.

Nevertheless check to see what each pupil knows or can do. See where they need extra help. Look at their strengths in the areas of literacy and numeracy. Then check how the class or school performed and where the pupil is placed within the group as well as in comparison with all other Year 3 pupils. Once again a knowledge of how to interpret test results is required and you should seek assistance. The worst thing to do is to just look at the bands—it is important that these are used for the benefit of each pupil.

Are the tests in Year 3 and Year 5 the same?

The tests increase in difficulty but the general content is much the same. Some questions might be repeated. This is to allow the test developers to standardise the results across Years 3 and 5. The similar questions act like anchors for all the other questions.

When are the tests held?

The tests are planned for May on an agreed date. The actual timetable is listed on the official website at www.nap.edu.au. They may be spread over several days. Ideally the tests should be given in the mornings.

How is NAPLAN related to *My School*?

The My School website reports the NAPLAN results for around 10 000 Australian schools. *My School* is available at www.myschool.edu.au.

Will children be shown what to do?

The testing program is normally very well organised with clear instructions for schools and teachers. Teachers receive special instructions for administering the tests.

Teachers will probably give children practice tests in the weeks before the NAPLAN Tests.

How our book's grading system works

Step 1

In this book you will notice that we have provided Check your skills pages. These pages provide you with information about the content of each question.

Step 2

Once you have completed the checklists you will be able to see the content that was easy for the student or the questions that were difficult.

How to proceed

We recommend that you sit with each student using this book or remain nearby to answer any questions or to provide encouragement. Do not leave them alone.

1. Start with the sample questions.

Work with each child. Explain to them how to answer a multiple-choice question. They may have never seen one previously. Tell them that they have to choose the correct answer. Explain that only one of the options is correct.

Show them how and where to write an answer if it is an open-ended question. Be patient if they do not understand at first.

2. Proceed to the practice tests.

Once you have covered the sample questions it is time to proceed to the practice tests. As we said previously these are deliberately short and gradually increase in length as the test stamina of the child increases. Do not attempt more than one practice test in one sitting. Remember that these are still young children and that they tire easily.

3. Stop when you reach the maximum level of performance.

When you realise that a child has reached their maximum level of performance in a practice test it is time to stop. Do not force children to try to go beyond their level. They may find it difficult because they might not have covered this content yet in Year 2. It may be beyond their natural ability at present and setting it aside for even a few months will allow them time to mature in their thinking and development. This is because there will be substantial increases in educational development, comprehension and understanding in Year 2. Some tasks that may be difficult at the outset will become easier later in the year. There will also be plenty of time to prepare in Year 3.

For pupils who find these tasks easy it is recommended that they move on to our *Excel Year 3 NAPLAN*-style Tests* book. This contains higher-level questions and longer tests.

• • • • • • • •

Please note that it is not possible to accurately predict the content of the NAPLAN Tests. NAPLAN focuses on the 'essential elements that should be taught at the appropriate year levels'.

Thank you for your patience in working through this introduction. We hope you find this guide helpful. It is designed to be easy to use and to help pupils prepare. We wish every pupil well in the NAPLAN Tests and in their future studies.

Associate Professor James A Athanasou, LittB, MA, PhD, DipEd, MAPS
Angella Deftereos, BA, MTeach

How is this book organised?

It is divided into sample questions and practice tests. We start with samples of the numeracy and literacy (reading and conventions of language) questions. Work through these examples so that every student knows what needs to be done. At the very least please ensure that your child is familiar with the sample questions.

This is followed by six practice tests for numeracy, six practice tests for reading and six practice tests for conventions of language. There is also a sample writing task and five practice tests for writing. At the very least try to revise the samples if you do not have enough time to do the practice tests.

The practice tests begin with very short and easy tasks. Then the length of the practice tests gradually increases, together with the difficulty of the questions.

We have done this mainly because of the young age of the children so that the tests do not become too tiring for them. We have also tried to group the questions into levels of difficulty so that the practice tests do not become too discouraging.

Numeracy Tests

The Numeracy Tests in this book have 10–36 questions. Allow around 1–2 minutes for each question in the Numeracy Test. So the first test should take up to 20 minutes. We allow around 45 minutes for the longest test. Some children will finish quickly while others will need all the time available.

Try not to explain terms during the testing. This can be done after the test session. If a question is still too hard, it is better to leave it at this stage. Some students may not be ready for the task.

Literacy Tests

Literacy is divided into three tests: Reading, Conventions of Language and Writing.

The Writing Test offers help with aspects of writing using prompts and stimulus materials.

Allow up to 45 minutes for Reading Tests, 45 minutes for Conventions of Language Tests and 40 minutes for Writing Tests, with a break in between.

- In the Reading Test students will read stories, letters and non-fiction writing. There will be supporting pictures and charts. Students will be asked to find information, make conclusions, find the meaning and look at different ideas.
- The Conventions of Language Test is divided into two parts: grammar and punctuation, and spelling. Students must be able to use verbs and punctuation, such as speech marks and commas, correctly. Also they will be asked to spell words.
- In the Writing Test students will write a specific type of text. They will be judged on the structure of their writing, as well as their grammar, punctuation and spelling.

Test materials

All test materials are contained in this book. There are answers for scoring the responses.

Equipment

Students will not need white-out, pens or calculators. It is best to use a pencil. Children should be provided with a pencil, an eraser and a blank sheet of paper for working out.

Time limits

Try to keep roughly to the time limits for the tests. You may give some students extra time if they are tired. Even a short break every 20 minutes is appropriate.

Instructions to students

Explain patiently what needs to be done. Students should only attempt these tests if they wish to and do no more than one test in a session.

Recording answers

Show students the way to mark the answers. They have to colour in circles, shapes or numbers, or write the answers in the boxes or on the lines provided.

There is a range of different types of sample Numeracy questions in this section. This way we can introduce you to a variety of question types so you have an idea of how to answer these different types.

If you aren't sure what to do, ask your teacher or your parents to help you. Don't be afraid to ask if it isn't clear to you. There is no time limit for the sample questions.

Types of questions where you colour in a circle for the answer (also called multiple-choice questions)

Example 1

Which of these groups shows the number 13?

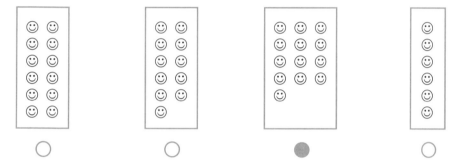

- See how we coloured in only **one** circle.
- When you answer these types of questions you have to colour in only one circle.
- Colour in the one you think is correct. If you change your mind, erase or rub out the old answer and colour in the new answer.

Example 2

How much are all these coins worth?

85c	$1.55	$1.75	$1.85
●	○	○	○

- See how we coloured in the **first** circle.
- You will notice that for many numeracy questions in the NAPLAN Test you will need to look at something first and then try to answer the question.

🖉 **Now try these questions. Remember to colour in only one circle.**

Sample question 1

Which number is the largest?

44	35	21	54
○	○	○	○

⭐ Did you colour in the **fourth** circle? **54** is the largest number.

Sample question 2

Which is the tallest person?

○	○	○	○

⭐ Did you colour in the **third** picture? Here is another practice question.

Sample question 3

Which shape is a triangle?

○	○	○	○

⭐ Did you colour in the **second** circle?

Here is a different type of question*. You have to read something and also look at a drawing carefully.

Sample question 4

I folded this pattern over the dotted black line.

Which shape could I see?

○   ○   ○

 This question might have been a little harder for you. Did you recognise the **second** one as the folded shape?

Sample question 5

Here are some pencils. Each child is given three pencils.

How many children will get three pencils?

3	4	5	6
○	○	○	○

 The answer was **4**. Did you colour in the **second** circle? There are 12 pencils and each child is given three. So there must be four children (3 + 3 + 3 + 3 = 12).

*Note: These tips for answering questions are provided to help your child become confident in completing the paper tests in this book.

Sample question 6

Here is a map which shows three towns on the edge of a lake. The map is divided into sections marked 1, 2, 3, 4 along the side and A, B, C, D along the bottom.

Which city is in C1?

Kangy Angy ○   Jetty Etty ○

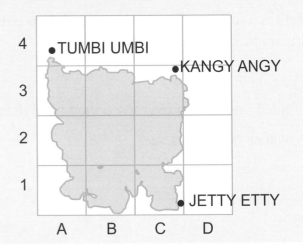

 Jetty Etty is at **C1**. Remember to count across the bottom first and then count upwards. If you don't know how to use grids, don't worry because there will be more questions like this to help you practise.

Where is Tumbi Umbi on the grid?

A1 ○   B4 ○   A4 ○   A3 ○

 Tumbi Umbi is in the square **A4**.

Types of questions where you write the answer

 In some questions you will need to write the answer. We have prepared some examples and sample questions for you.

Example 1

In our street there are five families. This table shows the number of children in each family.

Family	Number of children
Schilling	1
Athanasou	4
Schembri	3
Smith	1
Altiit	2

How many children do the Athanasou family and Schembri family have altogether?

7 children

Write your answer in the box.

The answer is **7** or **seven**. The Schembri family have three children and the Athanasou family have four children and this makes seven children altogether. See how we wrote our answer in the box provided.

Example 2

A drink costs $2. A mother buys three drinks. Fill in the number sentence below. Show how much she spent.

$$\$2 \times 3 = \$ \boxed{6}$$

 Write your answer in the box.

 The drink cost $2. The mother buys three drinks so the sum is $2 \times 3 = 6$.

 Here are some more questions where you need to write the answer. Are you ready?

Sample question 1

Use the calendar to answer the next question.

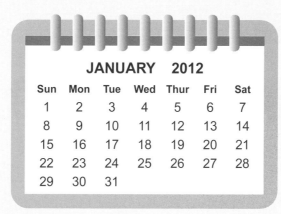

JANUARY 2012

Sun	Mon	Tue	Wed	Thur	Fri	Sat
1	2	3	4	5	6	7
8	9	10	11	12	13	14
15	16	17	18	19	20	21
22	23	24	25	26	27	28
29	30	31				

How many days are there from 11 to 25 January?

[   ] days

Write your answer in the box.

 The answer is **14** days. You can count the number of days on the calendar. There are 14 days from 11 to 25 January ($25 - 11 = 14$). Did you write your answer in the box?

Sample question 2

What time does this clock show?

Write your answer in the box.

 The answer is either **4:00** or **16:00** in digital time or **four o'clock**. Any of these answers is fine.

Sample question 3

Look at the picture on the right. The number zero looks the same when it is flipped or turned over sideways.

Now look at this picture. The number three is not the same when it is flipped or turned over sideways.

Which of these numbers will look the same if it is flipped or turned over sideways?

Write your answer in the box.

 ❽. The number ❽ looks the same when it is turned over sideways. This is what we mean by *flipped over*.

Sample question 4

There are 8 dollars to be divided. One person has to receive 4 dollars more than the other.

How much will each person get? Write your answer in the boxes.

[   ] dollars and [   ] dollars

Write your answer in the boxes.

 6 dollars and **2** dollars. This is because $6 + 2 = 8$ and the difference between them has to be four dollars.

Sample question 5

There is a pattern in these numbers. Write the number that is missing.

3   6   9   12   [   ]   18

Write your answer in the box.

 The pattern is 3, 6, 9, 12, **15**, then 18. The numbers are increasing by 3.

END OF QUESTIONS

How did you go with these sample questions? Are you confident that you know how to answer the different types of questions?

There are six Numeracy Tests to practise, starting with 10 questions. We gradually increase this to 36 questions. They include many different types of questions.

Here are some sample Reading questions. You will need to look at or read a text. Make sure you read each question carefully so that you know exactly what the question is asking. Then find the relevant section in the text. Finally make sure you read each answer option carefully in order to choose the correct answer. There is no time limit for the sample questions.

To answer these questions write the answer on the line or colour in the circle with the correct answer. Colour in only one circle for each answer.

If you aren't sure what to do, ask your teacher or your parents to help you. Don't be afraid to ask if it isn't clear to you.

Types of questions where you colour in a circle for the answer (also called multiple-choice questions)

Example

Look at this picture. It is from the cover of an old book.

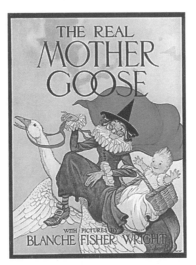

Source: Blanche Fisher Wright's cover artwork for the Rand McNally 1916 book *The Real Mother Goose*

What is the name of this book? Colour in only one of the answers.

- ○ Mother Goose
- ● The Real Mother Goose
- ○ Blanche Fisher Wright

- See how we coloured in only one circle.
- When you answer these types of questions you must colour in only **one** circle.
- Colour in the circle you think is correct. If you change your mind, rub out the old answer and colour in the new answer.

Now try this question. Remember to colour in only one circle.

Sample question 1

Look at this picture from the cover of a book.

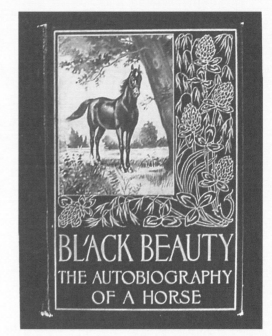

What is this book about?

- ○ It is a book about beauty.
- ○ It is a book about colours.
- ○ It is a book about a horse.

Source: http://www.oldchildrensbooks.com/books/
black-beauty-altemus-edition-19314

 Did you colour in the last answer? **It is a book about a horse.** Now we will give you some more examples of multiple-choice questions before you start. Ready?

Sample question 2

Read this description of some cartoon characters.

Bluegum is a fine, round, splendid fellow, with a tummy like a barrel. Uncle Bunyip is round, and his face has a moustache on it.

Which picture is Uncle Bunyip?

    ○   ○   ○   ○   ○

 This should have been easy for you. Did you colour in the **first** circle? It is the only one with a moustache. Now try another type of multiple-choice question.

Sample question 3

Here is a picture of a bicycle.

How many people can ride this bicycle?

two	three	four
○	○	○

 Did you colour in the circle next to **two**? This is a tandem cycle designed for two riders. That is why it has two sets of pedals, two seats and two handlebars.

Sample questions 4 to 9

Read this short story and then answer the questions.

Once upon a time there was a greedy dog. It ran off with a bone from a butcher's shop. The dog ran away as fast as it could. No one could catch it.

The dog kept on running and running. At last it came to a riverbank. It stopped for a moment and looked down into the water. It saw another dog with a large bone in its mouth.

The greedy dog thought, 'That dog has a bone that's as big as mine! I will jump on that dog and take its bone. Then I can have two bones.' But the silly dog did not realise that it was only seeing itself in the water.

The dog jumped in and there was a large splash of water but there was no other dog to be seen. As the greedy dog jumped in to grab the other bone, the bone that it had stolen dropped from its mouth. It sank down into the deep dark water.

Like all people who are greedy, there is nothing for them in the end. They end up with less.

There are six sample questions to answer.

4. What is the best way to describe the dog in this story?

naughty	greedy	angry
○	○	○

5. What did the dog see in the river?

a real dog	water	a mirror image of itself
○	○	○

6. What did the dog try to do?
   - ○ It wanted to fight the other dog.
   - ○ It jumped into the river.
   - ○ It tried to get another bone.

7. What happened to the dog?
   - ○ The dog found another dog.
   - ○ The dog tricked itself.
   - ○ The dog kept the bone.

8. What did the dog lose?
   - ○ The dog lost its temper.
   - ○ The dog lost the fight.
   - ○ The dog lost the bone.

9. What does this story teach us?
   - ○ It teaches us not to steal.
   - ○ It teaches us that greedy people can lose everything.
   - ○ It teaches us that greedy people are easy to fool.

⭐ Here are the answers to the sample questions:
   4. **greedy**
   5. **a mirror image of itself.** This is like a reflection.
   6. **It tried to get another bone.**
   7. **The dog tricked itself.**
   8. **The dog lost the bone.**
   9. **It teaches us that greedy people can lose everything.**

Types of questions where you write the answer

 In some questions you will need to write the answer. Here are some sample questions for you.

Sample question 1

Here is a road sign.

1. What is the meaning of this sign? Write your answer in the space provided.

 Over the next 4 km there may be a koala on the road. Any answer that has the same meaning is fine.

Sample questions 2 to 4

Look at this book cover.

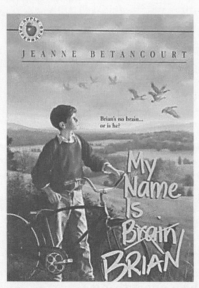

Source: Wikimedia Commons, http://commons.wikimedia.org/wiki/ File:My_name_is_brain_brian.jpg

2. Who is the author of this book? Write your answer on the line.

_____

3. What is the title of this book? Write your answer on the line.

_____

4. What might this book be about? Colour in the circle next to the answer that you think is correct.

○ bicycles

○ a boy who has trouble spelling but is quite clever

○ a boy who is called Brain

⭐ Here are the correct answers:

2. **Jeanne Betancourt**

3. **My name is ~~Brain~~ BRIAN**

4. **It might be about a boy who has trouble spelling but is quite clever.**
   Any equivalent or adequately justified answer is appropriate.

END OF QUESTIONS

How did you go with these sample questions? Are you confident that you know how to answer the different types of questions?

There are six Reading Tests to practise, starting with 10 questions. We gradually increase this to 39 questions. They include many of the same types of questions, plus a few other types.

Instructions for parents and teachers

This section tests whether students can spell words and find spelling, grammar and punctuation errors in a text.

The first series of questions are grammar and punctuation questions just as in NAPLAN Online. Then we have provided spelling words that are to be read out to the student. The words are read by a teacher or parent. The student writes their answer on the lines we have provided below. This is similar to NAPLAN Online.

Multiple-choice questions

Example 1

Show where a capital letter is needed. You can colour in more than one circle if you need to.

george went to melbourne in november and won't be back until christmas.

The correct answer is:

George went to Melbourne in November and won't be back until Christmas.

✏️ **Now try these questions. Remember to colour in only one circle on each line.**

Sample questions 1 and 2

Check the following sentences. Be careful: some sentences have more than one mistake.

Colour in the circles to show where an apostrophe is missing. You can colour in more than one circle.

1. Jims friends are very happy its the holidays.

2. They come to his fathers shop to see Jims new bike.

The correct answers are:

1. Jim's friends are very happy it's the holidays.
2. They come to his father's shop to see Jim's new bike.

Example 2

There are other types of questions in the NAPLAN Tests. In some questions the sentences have gaps. You have to colour in the circle next to the correct answer.

Friday [____] our sports day.

has	is	will
○	●	○

Sample questions 3 and 4

3. Sam was captain last [____].

weak	weke	week
○	○	○

4. Pat [____] her sneakers.

forgot	fourgot
○	○

 The correct answers are:

3. **week**
4. **forgot**

Types of questions where you write the answer

 In some questions you will need to write the answer. You may need to add punctuation.

Example

Show where the speech marks are needed. Write the correct sentence on the line.

"Good morning, said Mrs Jones.

_____

 You should have added a speech mark like this: "Good morning," said Mrs Jones.

We have underlined the change to make it easier for you to see.

Sample question 1

Show where an apostrophe is needed. Write the correct sentence on the line.

The dog wagged its tail at my sisters friends.

 You should have added an apostrophe, like this:

1. The dog wagged its tail at my sister**'s** friends.

We have underlined the change to make it easier for you to see.

Sample questions 2 and 3

Read the sentences. Find the mistakes and write the correct sentences on the lines. Be careful: some sentences have more than one mistake.

2. Jan came here from overseas. she said that she was happy to be in australia.

3. Henry help his mother shops at the supermarket.

 Here are the correct answers:

2. Jan came here from overseas. **S**he said that she was happy to be in **A**ustralia.

3. Henry <u>helps</u> his mother <u>shop</u> at the supermarket.

Sample spelling questions 4 to 11

To the teacher or parent

First read and say the word slowly and clearly. Then read the sentence with the word in it. Then repeat the word again.

If the student is not sure, ask them to guess. It is okay to skip a word if it is not known.

Sample spelling words

Word	Example
4. see	I can see a large truck.
5. only	I have only two stickers left.
6. any	There aren't any more ice-blocks left.
7. many	Many of my friends are going on holidays.
8. city	I love catching a bus with my mum to the city.
9. rain	I don't like the rain because we can't play outside.
10. party	I will have a party for my birthday in April.
11. our	Our cousins are playing soccer on Saturday.

Write your answer on the line.

4. _____

5. _____

6. _____

7. _____

8. _____

9. _____

10. _____

11. _____

Sample questions 12 to 14

The spelling mistakes in these sentences are underlined.

Write the correct spelling of each underlined word in the box.

12. A <u>mann</u> was pushed off his surfboard by a shark.

13. The shark was <u>arownd</u> three metres long.

14. There were <u>too</u> other large sharks.

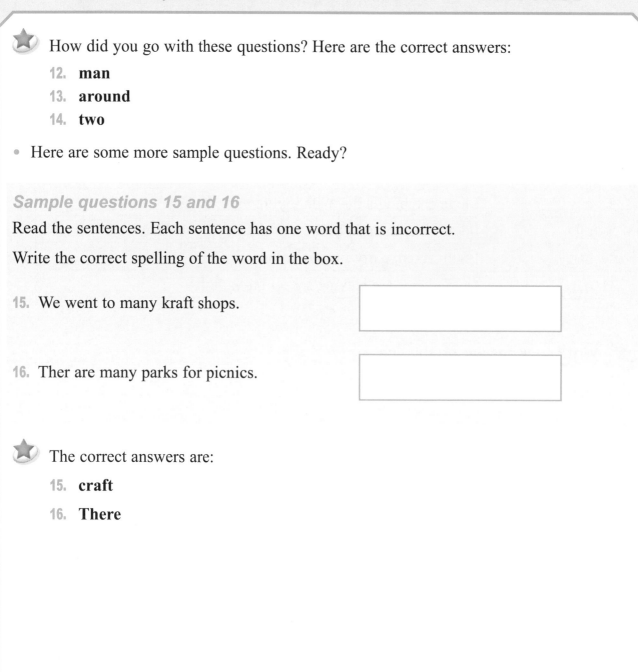

⭐ How did you go with these questions? Here are the correct answers:

12. **man**
13. **around**
14. **two**

• Here are some more sample questions. Ready?

Sample questions 15 and 16

Read the sentences. Each sentence has one word that is incorrect.

Write the correct spelling of the word in the box.

15. We went to many kraft shops.

16. Ther are many parks for picnics.

⭐ The correct answers are:

15. **craft**
16. **There**

END OF QUESTIONS

How did you go with these sample questions? Are you confident that you know how to answer the different types of questions?

There are six Conventions of Language Tests to practise, starting with 25 questions. We gradually increase this to 50 questions. They include many of the same types of questions, plus a few other types.

Now we're going to start the practice tests. Are you ready?

ADAPTED FOR
ONLINE
FORMAT

This is the first Numeracy Test. There are 10 questions.

If you aren't sure what to do, ask your teacher or your parents to help you. Don't be afraid to ask if it isn't clear to you.

Allow around 15 minutes for this test.

Write the answer in the box or colour in the circle with the correct answer. Colour in only one circle for each answer.

1. Which is the longest piece?

○

○

○

○

Did you colour in one of the circles?

....

2. Look at the ✶ shapes. Count how many. Then write how many TENS and ONES there are.

✶✶✶✶✶✶✶✶✶✶ ✶✶✶✶✶✶✶✶✶✶

✶✶✶✶✶✶✶✶✶✶ ✶

[ ] TENS [ ] ONES

Write your answer in the boxes.

....

3. Write these numbers from smallest to largest.

48   80   65   23   34

Start with the smallest number.

[ ] [ ] [ ] [ ] [ ]

Write your answer in the boxes.

4. What is the answer to this sum?

$$3 + 7 = ?$$

9	10	11	12
○	○	○	○

5. Look at this clock.

Which is the correct time?

7:00	8:00	9:00	10:00
○	○	○	○

6. Count the money.

How much are these coins worth altogether?

15 cents	25 cents	30 cents	40 cents
○	○	○	○

☞ Tip for Question 7

Let us start with an example to help you. Here is a number sentence and also a sum for that sentence.

Example

Number sentence $10 + 10 + 10 + 10$

Sum $4 \times 10 = 40$

7. Here is another number sentence.

Number sentence $5 + 5 + 5 + 5 + 5 + 5$

Which is the correct sum for this sentence?

$6 \times 5 = 30$ $5 \times 5 = 25$ $6 \times 5 = 35$ $5 \times 5 = 30$
○   ○   ○   ○

8. Count the crayons. Each child is given three crayons.

How many children will get crayons?

3   4   5   6
○   ○   ○   ○

9. This is a picture of a supermarket shelf.

What is between the cheese and the butter?

eggs   yoghurt   pizza   milk
○   ○   ○   ○

> ☞ **Tip for Question 10**

Let us start with an example to help you. Here are some numbers. They are in order but some numbers have been left out of the picture.

Example

What is missing?   ☐ 2 ☐ 4 5 ☐ 7 8 ☐ 10

Write the missing numbers.   1 2 3 4 5 6 7 8 9 10

10. Now here is another set of numbers. Write the numbers that are missing.

☐ 37 ☐ 39 40 ☐ 42 43 ☐ 45

> **Write your answer in the boxes.** ✏

- -

END OF TEST

You have done quite well if you managed to complete all these questions. Even if you do not complete any other tests then at least you will have practised a fair sample of the type of questions in a Numeracy Test.

How did you go with these test questions? Some questions might have been easy for you. There might have been questions that you haven't learnt in class yet or others that were a little harder. We apologise if too many of the questions were different to those you are used to but you can use these questions and their answers to help you learn. Check to see which questions you did well in and which questions you had some problems with. Perhaps you could revise the questions that were hard for you with a parent or teacher.

Use the chart on page 24 to see what level of performance you reached. Again we remind you that this level will only be an estimate of your performance. Don't be surprised if you answered some difficult questions correctly or even missed some easier questions.

There are now five more Numeracy Tests to practise. The next test contains 15 questions. We will include new types of questions in each of the tests.

Instructions

Check the answers

As you check the answer for each question, mark it as correct (✓) or incorrect (✗). Mark any questions that you omitted or left out as incorrect (✗) for the moment.

Then look at how many you answered correctly in each level. Your level of ability is the point where you started having consistent difficulty with questions. For example, if you answered most questions correctly at the Standard level and then got most questions wrong from then onwards, it is likely your ability is at a Standard level. You can ask your parents or your teacher to help you do this if it isn't clear.

We expect you to miss some easy questions and also to answer some hard questions correctly, but your level of ability should be where you are starting to find the questions too hard. Some students will reach the top level—this means that their ability cannot be measured by these questions or even the NAPLAN Tests. They found it far too easy.

Understanding the different levels

We have divided the questions into three levels of difficulty:

* Standard
* Intermediate
* Advanced.

For each question we have described the skill involved in answering the question. Then, depending on what sort of skill is involved, we have placed it into one of the three levels. It should make sense, especially when you go back and look at the type of question. The Standard level includes the easiest tasks and then they increase in difficulty.

The purpose of these practice tests is to help you be as confident as possible and perform to the best of your ability. The purpose of the NAPLAN Tests is to show what you know or can do. For the first time the user can estimate their level of ability before taking the actual test and see if there is any improvement across the practice tests.

Remember that the levels of ability are only a rough guide. No claim is made that they are perfect. They are only an indicator. Your level might change as you do each practice test. We hope that these brief notes are of some help.

Instructions

- As you check the answer for each question, mark it as correct (✓) or incorrect (✗).
- Mark any questions that you missed or left out as incorrect (✗) for the moment.
- Go back and practise the questions you missed out or got incorrect. You can ask your parents or your teacher to help you do this if it isn't clear to you.
- For this first test we have only given you one level of questions to begin with.
- For the rest of the tests you will be given more levels of questions and you will be able to work out approximately what level your performance is.

Am I able to ...

	SKILL	ESTIMATED LEVEL	✓ or ✗
1	Compare the length of objects by observation?	Standard	
2	Write the number of tens and ones to match the number of objects?	Standard	
3	Write five two-digit numbers from smallest to largest?	Standard	
4	Add two single-digit numbers together?	Standard	
5	Convert analog to digital time?	Standard	
6	Add the value of three coins?	Standard	
7	Write a sum for a number sentence?	Standard	
8	Divide a quantity into groups?	Standard	
9	Describe the position of objects in drawings using everyday language?	Standard	
10	Complete a number sequence?	Standard	
	TOTAL		

This is the second Numeracy Test. There are 15 questions.
There are five more questions than in Test 1.

If you aren't sure what to do, ask your teacher or your parents to help you.
Don't be afraid to ask if it isn't clear to you.

Allow around 20 minutes for this test.

Write the answer in the box or colour in the circle with the correct answer.
Colour in only one circle for each answer.

1. Which number is largest?

$$642 \qquad 462 \qquad 624 \qquad 246$$

○ ○ ○ ○

2. Which object is a cylinder?

○ ○ ○

3. What is the answer to this sum?

$$13 + 3 + 4 = \boxed{}$$

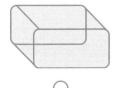

Write your answer in the box.

4. How much of this shape is coloured?

one-third   two-thirds   three-quarters   one-half

○ ○ ○ ○

5. This table shows the number of points five countries won in a football competition.

Team	Number of points
Australia	7
South Korea	5
Bahrain	6
Saudi Arabia	1
Qatar	4

Which team is in third place?

South Korea   Bahrain   Saudi Arabia   Qatar

○   ○   ○   ○

6. How will the weight of this bag of flour be measured?

in kilograms   in litres   in metres   in minutes

○   ○   ○   ○

7. Show the time for 3:30 on this clock.

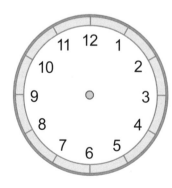

8. Here are the prices at the local shop.

TONY'S FRUIT SHOP
WEEKLY SPECIALS

APPLE 50c	BANANA 35c	CHERRY 20c	LEMON 45c
PINEAPPLE $1.90	PEAR 35c	TOMATO 25c	CORN 85c
PUMPKIN $2.50	WATERMELON $5	KIWI FRUIT 95c	AVOCADO 65c

Ahmed buys one pear, one kiwi fruit and one banana. How much does he spend?

$1.65 $5.75 $3.85 $4.15
○   ○   ○   ○

9. Add these numbers.

$$\begin{array}{r} 3\ 6 \\ +\ 2\ 4 \\ \hline \end{array}$$

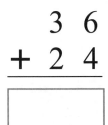

Write your answer in the box.

---

10. This chart shows three faces. They are at different spots in the chart. The chart is divided into sections marked 1, 2, 3 along the side and A, B, C along the bottom.

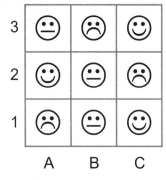

Which picture is in B2?

  ○   ○   ○

---

11. Here is a line. Estimate or guess its length.

5 cm   14 cm   30 cm   50 cm
  ○   ○   ○   ○

12. Which of these shapes will **not** look the same if it is flipped (horizontally) or turned over sideways?

Remember to look for the one that is **not** the same.

○   ○   ○

---

13. What number should come next in this pattern?

38   36   34   32   30   ?

28   29   31   27

○   ○   ○   ○

---

14. In this map there are three pathways. Along the way you add or subtract some numbers.

Which pathway—A, B or C—will give you 15?

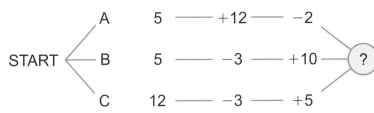

A   B   C

○   ○   ○

15. Move the dot along the shaded path. How many moves will the dot need to make to reach the end? (You can only move one space at a time.)

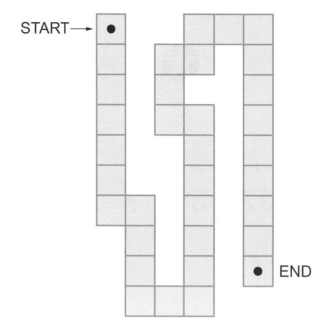

START→

END

The total number of moves is

less than 23.   less than 26.   less than 39.   more than 40.

○   ○   ○   ○

· ·

END OF TEST

How did you go with these test questions? Some were probably still easy questions for you. There might have been some questions that you have not yet learnt in class and these may have been a little harder. Again we apologise if too many of the questions were a little different. It is hard to know what will suit every student but you can use these questions to help you learn. Check to see where you did well and where you had problems. Try to revise the questions that were hard for you.

Use the chart on page 31 to see which level of performance you reached. Again we remind you that this is only an estimate. Don't be surprised if you answered some difficult questions correctly or even missed some easier questions.

There are now four more Numeracy Tests to practise. The next test contains 20 questions. We will include other types of questions in each of the tests.

Instructions

- As you check the answer for each question, mark it as correct (✓) or incorrect (✘). Mark any questions that you omitted or left out as incorrect (✘) for the moment.
- Then look at how many questions you answered correctly in each level.
- You will be able to see what level you are at by finding the point where you started having consistent difficulty with questions at a certain level. For example, if you answered most questions correctly up to the Intermediate level, it is likely your ability is at the Intermediate level. You can ask your parents or your teacher to help you do this if it isn't clear to you.

Am I able to ...

	SKILL	ESTIMATED LEVEL	✓ or ✘
1	Compare numbers to find the largest?	Standard	
2	Identify a cylinder?	Standard	
3	Add three numbers equal to 20?	Standard	
4	Identify the fraction of a figure?	Standard	
5	Locate data in a table?	Standard	
6	Identify kilogram as a measure of weight?	Standard	
7	Draw the time on a clockface?	Standard	
8	Add the value of three items in shopping?	Intermediate	
9	Add two-digit numbers?	Intermediate	
10	Locate a cell in a two-way chart?	Intermediate	
11	Estimate the length of a line?	Intermediate	
12	Flip a shape horizontally?	Intermediate	
13	Complete a number series decreasing by two?	Intermediate	
14	Follow a pathway of addition and subtraction to a total?	Intermediate	
15	Estimate an inequality?	Intermediate	
	TOTAL		

This is the third Numeracy Test. There are 20 questions.
There are five more questions than in Test 2.

If you aren't sure what to do, ask your teacher or your parents to help you.
Don't be afraid to ask if it isn't clear to you.

Allow around 25 minutes for this test.

Write the answer in the box or colour in the circle with the correct answer.
Colour in only one circle for each answer.

1. Here are some billiard balls. There are 6 balls in each group.

   Count the number of billiard balls.

   How many billiard balls are there altogether?

   Did you colour in one of the circles?

   10　　　　　15　　　　　18　　　　　20
   ○　　　　　○　　　　　○　　　　　○

2. Here is something we want you to guess.

   About how many people are likely to live in our house?

   You do not know the exact answer but we want you to guess the likely number.

   0　　　　4　　　　14　　　　24　　　　40
   ○　　　　○　　　　○　　　　○　　　　○

3. Which time matches 6:15?

   ○　　　　　○　　　　　○　　　　　○

4. What is the answer to this sum?

$$18 \div 2 = \boxed{}$$

Write your answer in the box.

---

5. Here is another sum.

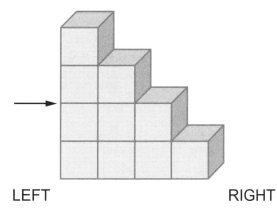

$$\begin{array}{r} 1\ 2 \\ \times\quad 3 \\ \hline \end{array}$$

What is the answer?

24	26	32	36
○	○	○	○

---

6. Here is a solid shape.

LEFT   RIGHT

If you look at this shape from the **left**, what outline will you see?

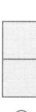      

○   ○   ○

7. Imagine a long piece of wood. This is measured by a tape or ruler.

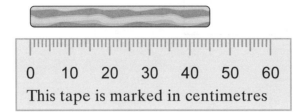

This tape is marked in centimetres

About how long is this piece of wood?

40 cm	45 cm	50 cm	55 cm
○	○	○	○

8. Here are some sheep in a paddock.

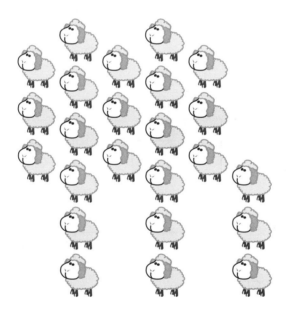

Divide them into three equal groups.

How many are there in each group?

6	7	8	9
○	○	○	○

9. Below is a ticket for an order at a fish shop.

The order number on this receipt has been circled.
What would the next order number be?

○ 4210

○ 403

○ 430

○ 420

THE FISH MARKET
@ MAROUBRA
789 ANZAC PDE
MAROUBRA JUNCTION NSW 2035
PH: 8931 5684

THE FISH MARKET @ MAROUBRA
TAX INVOICE
ABN 12 345 678 910

26/01/2011 06:58 pm   Invoice # 14517
Server: NICK   TILL 1

ORDER NUMBER
429

Invoice Ttl $19.70

GST $1.79
Paid CASH $50.00
Change $30.30

YOUR RECIEPT
THANK YOU

---

10. Here is a subtraction. What number is missing?

$$30 - \boxed{} = 9$$

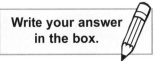

Write your answer in the box.

---

11. There is a pattern in these numbers but three are missing.

27   21 18   12 9 6   0

Which three numbers are missing?

24, 16, 2	23, 16, 3	24, 15, 3	22, 16, 2
	○	○	○

---

12. Here is a sheet of coloured paper.

Petra cut this shape out of the coloured paper.

Which shape should Petra see? (Hint: the shape can be moved around.)

   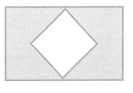

○   ○   ○   ○

---

13. My watch shows the following time: `9:00`

My bedroom clock shows:

How many minutes are there between the two times?

30 minutes	15 minutes	60 minutes	6 minutes
○	○	○	○

14. Look at these scales.

They show the weight of something.

Which answer is correct?

○ The weight is more than 8 kg and less than 9 kg.

○ The weight is more than 5 kg and less than 7 kg.

○ The weight is more than 7 kg and less than 8 kg.

15. Which shape below has only 1 line of symmetry?

○ ○ ○ ○

16. Mikee made this shape using the same-sized blocks.

Which number sentence shows how he would work out the total number of blocks he used?

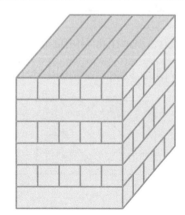

○ 5 × 6

○ 5 × 10

○ 5 + 5 + 5 + 10

○ 6 × 6 + 5

17. How many quarters are there in two and a half oranges?

3	4	8	10	12
○	○	○	○	○

18. Here is a cupboard.

There is a top, middle and bottom row.

There are six places on each row.

We have shown the places on each row with a letter.

TOP ROW	A	B	C	D	E	F
MIDDLE ROW	G	H	I	J	K	L
BOTTOM ROW	M	N	O	P	Q	R

Place a cross (✖) third from the right in the top row.

In which space is it placed?

Write your answer in the box.

19. Nicholas bought a kebab for $7 and a falafel roll for $8. He gave the shop assistant $20. How much change did he receive?

$3	$4	$5	$6	$7
○	○	○	○	○

20. This square is made up of the numbers from 1 to 9.

9	?	1	=15
4	?	8	=15
2	?	6	=15

=15   =15   =15

In this square all the numbers across and down come to the same total.

For each row (across) the total is 15. For each column (down) the total is also 15.

There is one column missing. Find these values and write them in the missing spaces below.

9		1
4		8
2		6

Write your answer in the boxes.

END OF TEST

How did you go with these test questions? Some were probably still easy questions for you. There might have been some questions that you have not yet learnt in class and these may have been a little harder. Remember that you can use these questions to help you learn. Check to see where you did well and where you had problems. Try to revise the questions that were hard for you.

Use the chart on page 39 to see which level of performance you reached. Again we remind you that this is only an estimate. Don't be surprised if you answered some difficult questions correctly or even missed some easier questions.

There are now three more Numeracy Tests to practise. The next test contains 25 questions. We will include other types of questions in each of the following tests.

Instructions

- As you check the answer for each question, mark it as correct (✓) or incorrect (✗). Mark any questions that you omitted or left out as incorrect (✗) for the moment.
- Then look at how many questions you answered correctly in each level.
- You will be able to see what level you are at by finding the point where you started having consistent difficulty with questions at a certain level. For example, if you answered most questions correctly up to the Intermediate level and then got most questions wrong from then onwards, it is likely your ability is at the Intermediate level. You can ask your parents or your teacher to help you do this if it isn't clear to you.

Am I able to ...

	SKILL	ESTIMATED LEVEL	✓ or ✗
1	Count the number of items in three groups?	Standard	
2	Estimate a likely number?	Standard	
3	Match the time and a clockface?	Standard	
4	Divide a two-digit number less than 20 by 2?	Standard	
5	Multiply a two-digit number less than or equal to 12 by 3?	Standard	
6	Describe the side view of a solid?	Standard	
7	Measure the length of an object?	Intermediate	
8	Divide a group of objects into 4?	Intermediate	
9	Identify the next number after a given 3-digit number?	Intermediate	
10	Insert a missing value into a subtraction?	Intermediate	
11	Complete a number series decreasing by 3?	Intermediate	
12	Match a figure with a section missing?	Intermediate	
13	Compare time on the hour and half hour using digital and analog clocks?	Intermediate	
14	Judge the truth of the range of a value?	Intermediate	
15	Find all lines of symmetry for 2D shapes?	Intermediate	
16	Calculate the volume of a prism?	Advanced	
17	Find the number of quarters in two and a half objects?	Advanced	
18	Locate an object in a row and column?	Advanced	
19	Solve a two-step problem involving addition then subtraction?	Advanced	
20	Complete a number square?	Advanced	
	TOTAL		

An important note about the NAPLAN Online tests

The NAPLAN Online Numeracy test will be divided into different sections. Students will only have one opportunity to check their answers at the end of each section before proceeding to the next one. This means that after students have completed a section and moved onto the next they will not be able to check their work again. We have included reminders for students to check their work at specific points in the practice tests from now on so they become familiar with this process.

This is the fourth Numeracy Test. There are 25 questions.
There are five more questions than in Test 3.

If you aren't sure what to do, ask your teacher or your parents to help you.
Don't be afraid to ask if it isn't clear to you.

Allow around 30 minutes for this test.

Write the answer in the box or colour in the circle with the correct answer.
Colour in only one circle for each answer.

A girl and a boy have some books.

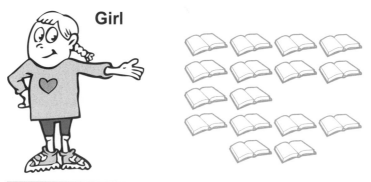

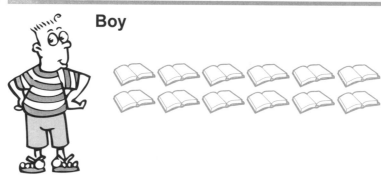

1. Who has more books?

   ○ The girl has more books.

   ○ The boy has more books.

2. How many books are there altogether?

22	24	26	28	30
○	○	○	○	○

3. What part or fraction of this shape is coloured?

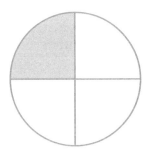

three-quarters   one-quarter   half
   ○   ○   ○

4. Which coins can we use to make 45 cents?

50c, 10c   5c, 10c, 20c   20c, 20c, 5c
  ○   ○   ○

5. One child has three paintbrushes.

Another child has five paintbrushes.

Which sum shows how many paintbrushes there are altogether?

$3 + 5 = 9$ $8 - 5 = 3$ $3 + 5 = 7$ $3 + 5 = 8$
  ○   ○   ○   ○

6. This is part of the timetable for the 394 and 396 buses. It shows the time, the bus number and where the bus is going.

Time	Bus number	Destination
9:00 am	394	La Perouse
9:15 am	396	Maroubra Beach
9:30 am	394	La Perouse
9:45 am	396	Maroubra Beach
10:00 am	394	La Perouse
10:15 am	396	Maroubra Beach
10:30 am	394	La Perouse
10:45 am	396	Maroubra Beach
11:00 am	394	La Perouse

If the time is 9:50 am, when is the next 396 bus to Maroubra Beach?

10:30 am	10:15 am	9:45 am	10:00 am
○	○	○	○

7. Here is a chart of a desert area. It is filled with camels, cacti and also a well. They are at different spots on the chart. The chart is divided into sections marked 1, 2, 3 along the bottom and A, B, C along the side.

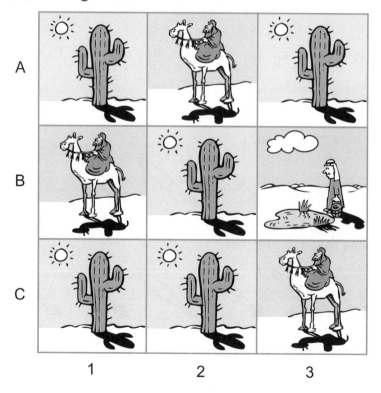

Which picture is in A2?

cactus

camel

well

8. In which section is the well?

C2	B1	B2	B3
○	○	○	○

☞ **Tip for Question 9**

Before we start the next question we want to make sure you know something about directions. The main directions on a map are North, South, East and West. They are shown in this chart. It may help you answer the next three questions.

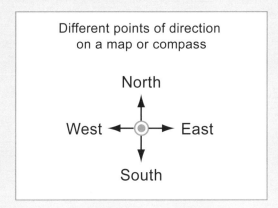

Different points of direction
on a map or compass

9. Which direction on any map is the opposite of North? (Don't worry if you haven't been taught this yet.)

South	East	West	North
○	○	○	○

Here is a map of an area we often visit. It shows some towns around a lake. The direction of North is shown.

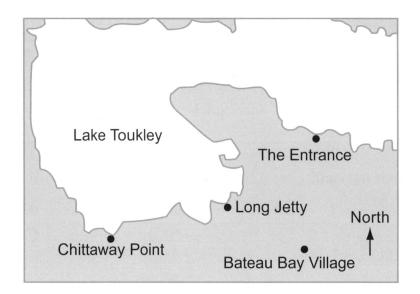

10. Which town is the most northern on this map?

  ○ Bateau Bay Village

  ○ Chittaway Point

  ○ Long Jetty

  ○ The Entrance

11. In which direction would you travel if you went from Bateau Bay Village to The Entrance?

North	South	East	West
○	○	○	○

12. What number is missing from this sum?

13 + 7 = 11 + ☐?

7	8	9	10	11
○	○	○	○	○

It would be a good idea to check your answers to questions 1 to 12 before moving on to the other questions.

13. There is a pattern in this series of numbers.

| 23 | 25 | 27 | 29 | 31 | ? |

Which number comes next in this series?

[   ]

Write your answer
in the box.

---

14. Here is a bottle of medicine.

How will this medicine be measured?

- ○ in millilitres
- ○ in litres
- ○ in degrees
- ○ in kilograms
- ○ in grams
- ○ in centimetres

☞ Tip for Question 15

Here is an example of some letters which have been flipped vertically (that is, turned over).

Example

M N O P   Original

W N O b   Turned over/
Flipped vertically

Only one letter (O) kept the same shape and the others (M N P) did not.

---

15. Which one of these letters will **not** look the same if it is flipped vertically or turned over?

A   C   D   E

○   ○   ○   ○

---

16. How many 10-cent coins would be needed to make up $1.50?

12   13   14   15

○   ○   ○   ○

---

17. How long is an hour?

30 seconds   30 minutes   60 seconds   60 minutes

○   ○   ○   ○

18. Ginger had some money in her pocket. She bought two cookies and a bottle of drink for $3.10 and then had $1.90 left.

How much did she start with?

> **Write your answer in the box.**

---

19. Answer this sum.

$$\begin{array}{r} 2\ 3 \\ \times\quad 5 \\ \hline \end{array}$$

> **Write your answer in the box.**

---

20. Answer this sum.

$2 \times 7 + 5 - 4 =$ ☐ ?

45   21   15

◯   ◯   ◯

21. Look at this chart. It shows the types of boats available at the boatshed.

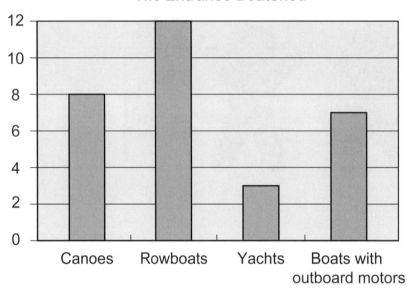

The Entrance Boatshed

Which answer is correct?

○ There are more rowboats than canoes and boats with outboard motors.

○ There are more rowboats than canoes and yachts.

○ There are more boats with outboard motors and yachts than there are rowboats.

○ There are more rowboats than there are boats with outboard motors plus canoes.

22. Josie took her dog, Wally, to the vet on 6 August. Wally has to go back to the vet in exactly 3 weeks. When will Wally next have to visit the vet? Use the calendar below to help you.

AUGUST 2012						
SUN	MON	TUE	WED	THU	FRI	SAT
			1	2	3	4
5	6	7	8	9	10	11
12	13	14	15	16	17	18
19	20	21	22	23	24	25
26	27	28	29	30	31	

27 August	26 August	20 August	9 August
○	○	○	○

23. The sides of a dice show six numbers, from 1 to 6. We can throw the dice and it will land on one of its sides.

If we throw this dice, what is the chance it will land on the side with the number 4?

○ 1 out of 6 chances

○ 4 out of 6 chances

○ 6 out of 4 chances

○ 4 out of 4 chances

24. Here are three sets of dots. There is a pattern. To find the last column in each row you need to look at the other two. Write the number of dots that will complete the pattern.

ROW 1	●	● ● ●	● ● ● ●
ROW 2	● ●	● ● ● ●	● ● ● ● ● ●
ROW 3	● ● ●	● ● ● ● ●	?

> **Write your answer in the box.**

> ☞ **Tip for Question 25**

An estimate is your best guess. It can be the closest answer to a question.

Example

For the sum 168 + 41 an estimate could be around 210. The correct answer is 209.

Why did we pick 210? We sort of guessed—to help you add quickly you can round off or change the numbers to end in a '0'. This will make them easy to add and also to guess.

168 becomes 170.

41 becomes 40.

The estimated sum would be: 170 + 40 = 210. The answer of 210 is fairly close but not perfectly accurate. It is an estimate.

To help you estimate there are two rules.

Rule 1

If a number ends in 1 or 2 or 3 or 4, change or round it down to end in a zero.

Rule 2

If a number ends in 5 or more, change or round it up to the next 0. (There are some more complicated rules but we will use only these two for now.)

25. Now estimate the answer to this sum:

$$37 + 12 = \boxed{?}$$

30	40	50	60
○	○	○	○

END OF TEST

How did you go with these test questions? Some were probably harder questions for you. There might have been some questions that you have not yet learnt in class but you can use these questions to help you learn. Check to see where you did well and where you had problems. Try to revise the questions that were hard for you.

Use the chart on page 51 to see which level of performance you reached. Again we remind you that this is only an estimate. Don't be surprised if you answered some difficult questions correctly or even missed some easier questions.

There are now two more Numeracy Tests to practise. The next test contains 30 questions. We will include other types of questions in each of the tests.

Instructions

- As you check the answer for each question, mark it as correct (✓) or incorrect (✗). Mark any questions that you omitted or left out as incorrect (✗) for the moment.

- Then look at how many questions you answered correctly in each level.

- You will be able to see what level you are at by finding the point where you started having consistent difficulty with questions at a certain level. For example, if you answered most questions correctly up to the Intermediate level and then got most questions wrong from then onwards, it is likely your ability is at the Intermediate level. You can ask your parents or your teacher to help you do this if it isn't clear to you.

Am I able to ...

	SKILL	ESTIMATED LEVEL	✓ or ✗
1	Recognise a greater quantity?	Standard	
2	Calculate a total of two amounts?	Standard	
3	Recognise a quarter of a whole figure?	Standard	
4	Calculate the value of some coins?	Standard	
5	Recognise a number sentence for a single-digit addition?	Standard	
6	Calculate time in a timetable?	Standard	
7	Locate position by using coordinates on a grid?	Standard	
8	Locate position by using coordinates on a grid?	Standard	
9	State the opposite of north from a diagram?	Intermediate	
10	Find the most northern town on a map?	Intermediate	
11	State the direction of travel?	Intermediate	
12	Find a value to complete two sides of an addition equation?	Intermediate	
13	Complete a series of odd numbers?	Intermediate	
14	Select millilitres as a unit for medicines?	Intermediate	
15	Compare a shape with one that has been flipped vertically?	Intermediate	
16	Determine the number of coins needed for an amount?	Intermediate	
17	Recall that there are 60 minutes in an hour?	Intermediate	
18	Calculate starting amount of money after being given amount spent and amount remaining?	Advanced	
19	Multiply a two-digit number by a single digit?	Advanced	
20	Follow order of operations with multiplication first?	Advanced	
21	Deduce a conclusion from data in a chart?	Advanced	
22	Count forward on a calendar to identify the correct date?	Advanced	
23	Estimate the chance of a throw of a dice?	Advanced	
24	Complete a number sequence?	Advanced	
25	Estimate the solution to an addition?	Advanced	
	TOTAL		

This is the fifth Numeracy Test. There are 30 questions.
There are five more questions than in Test 4.

If you aren't sure what to do, ask your teacher or your parents to help you.
Don't be afraid to ask if it isn't clear to you.

Allow around 40 minutes for this test.

Write the answer in the box or colour in the circle with the correct answer.
Colour in only one circle for each answer.

1. Look at the grey shapes in this picture.

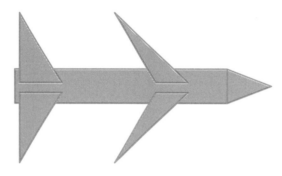

Which two different types of grey shapes are used in this picture?

triangle, square	triangle, rectangle	square, rectangle	cube, triangle
◯	◯	◯	◯

2. Here is the number **632**.

How many hundreds, tens and units are there in this number?

[   ] HUNDREDS   [   ] TENS   [   ] UNITS

> Write your answer in the boxes.

3. What is the answer to this sum?

$$22 \div 2 = \boxed{\ ?\ }$$

9	10	11	12
◯	◯	◯	◯

4. Draw a line along the top of this ruler. Make the line 7 cm long.

   Start your line from this dot.

   •

   | 0 | 1 | 2 | 3 | 4 | 5 | 6 | 7 | 8 | 9 | 10 |
   cm

5. Which pair of numbers shows a number that is 10 more than 498 and a number that is 10 less than 498?

	Ten more than 498	Ten less than 498
○	478	508
○	488	508
○	508	488
○	508	478

6. Which time best matches 4:15?

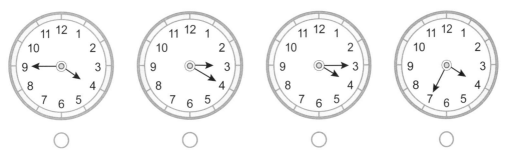

   ○   ○   ○   ○

7. Here are some tyres.

   Share them into three equal groups. How many are left over?

   4   3   2   1

   ○   ○   ○   ○

8. The shapes below are the faces of a 3D shape. What is the name of the shape?

○ triangular pyramid

○ triangular prism

○ rectangular pyramid

○ rectangular prism

9. The water in this jug is shown as grey. There is a scale in millilitres (mL) to help you see the amount of water.

```
        mL
1000
 800
 600
 400
 200
```

How much water is in this jug?

[   ] mL

Write your answer in the box.

10. The table below lists how many flowers of different types are in my garden.

FLOWERS IN MY GARDEN	
Flower	Number
Rose	2
Daisy	8
Lily	12
Camellia	4

How many lilies and daisies are there in my garden altogether?

10	16	20	24
○	○	○	○

Here is a map of our local area. It shows the main roads. It shows the suburbs of Maroubra and Kingsford. There is also the university and my old school.

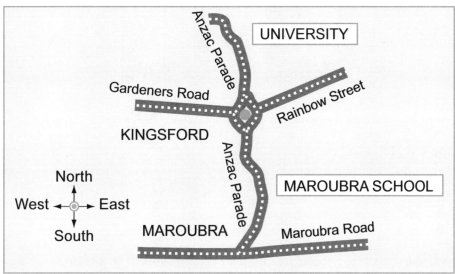

11. Is the school North, South, East or West of the university? Use the directions on the side of the map to help you.

North	South	East	West
○	○	○	○

12. Is Gardeners Road to the North, South, East or West of Anzac Parade? Use the directions on the side of the map to help you.

North	South	East	West
○	○	○	○

13. A bunch of tulips has six flowers.

Look at the number of tulips in the drawing below.

How many bunches with six flowers can be made?

4	5	6	7
○	○	○	○

14. Ben cut a white shape out of the green paper. Then he folded the paper in half.

FOLD HERE

Which shape did Ben see?

○   ○   ○

15. Look at these two ropes. The first one is around 15 cm long. The second rope is about 4 cm long.

How much longer is the top rope?

11 cm	12 cm	13 cm	14 cm
○	○	○	○

It would be a good idea to check your answers to questions 1 to 15 before moving on to the other questions.

16. A toffee apple costs $1. A candy bar costs 50 cents.

How much will two toffee apples and a candy bar cost?

○ $3.00

○ $2.50

○ $3.50

○ $4.00

17. What is the next number in the number pattern?

50   47   44   41   38   35   32

Write your answer in the box.

18. Here is a chart of rainfall across different towns. This is counted in millilitres.

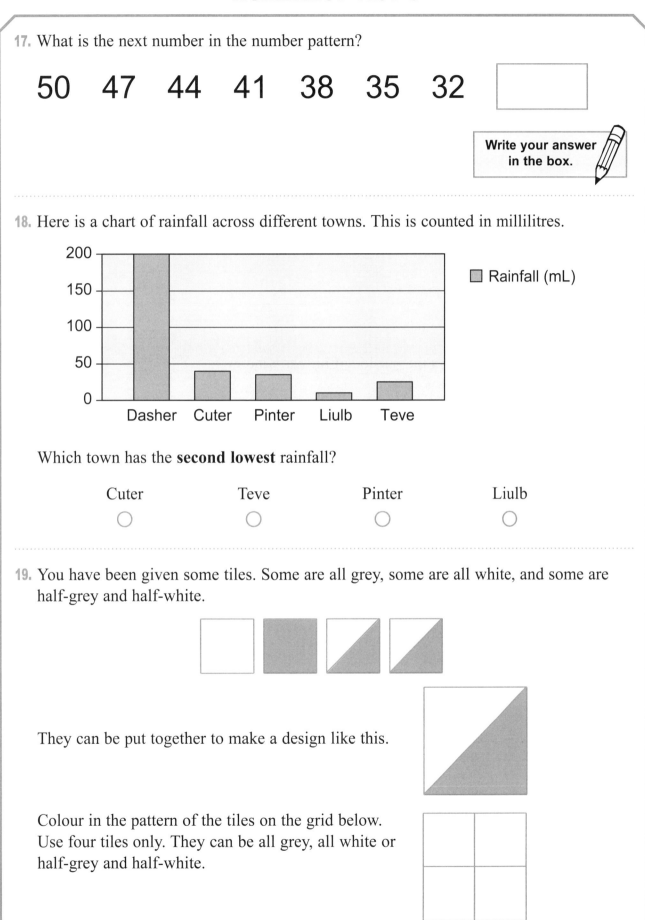

Which town has the **second lowest** rainfall?

Cuter   Teve   Pinter   Liulb
  ○   ○   ○   ○

19. You have been given some tiles. Some are all grey, some are all white, and some are half-grey and half-white.

They can be put together to make a design like this.

Colour in the pattern of the tiles on the grid below. Use four tiles only. They can be all grey, all white or half-grey and half-white.

20. Here is a square pyramid. You cannot see all the sides.

How many edges are there on this square pyramid? (Hint: don't count the sides. Only count the edges.)

5	8	10	12
○	○	○	○

21. Lucky stuck this sticker on the outside of his car window.

What does the sticker look like from inside his car window?

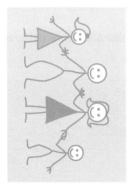

22. $100 + 90 + 5 = ?$

100 905	1 905	10 095	195
○	○	○	○

This table shows when some children lived in our street.

Years	Child
2000–2010	Graham
2005–2011	Mark
2002–2009	Gail
2000–2011	Ann
2004–2011	Ronnie
2006–2011	Dawn

23. Who lived in the street for the longest time?

Graham	Mark	Gail	Ann	Ronnie	Dawn
○	○	○	○	○	○

24. Which answer is correct?

○ Ronnie lived in the street longer than Graham.

○ Mark lived in the street longer than Ronnie.

○ Graham lived in the street longer than Ann.

○ Gail lived in the street longer than Dawn.

25. This is a chart showing the same information in a different way.

The children are now called A, B, C, D, E and F.

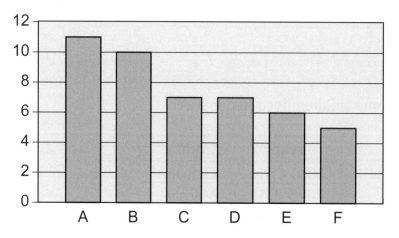

For how many years has child E lived in the street?

 years

Write your answer in the box.

What is the name of child E? (Hint: you will also need to look at the table in Question 23.)

Write your answer in the box.

26. A plane trip to London from Australia costs about $1800.

How would you work out the cost of four tickets to London?

Would you

- ○ divide $1800 by 4?
- ○ add 4 to $1800?
- ○ subtract 4 from $1800?
- ○ multiply $1800 by 4?

27. Which answer is true?

- ○ There are more odd numbers than even numbers.
- ○ Some odd numbers can be divided evenly by two.
- ○ An even number is an odd number plus one.

28. Nicholas plays cricket on Saturday. He plays cricket tomorrow. Which of these is certain?

- ○ Nicholas will bowl first.
- ○ He will get out after 9 runs.
- ○ Two from the team will be away.
- ○ Today is Friday.

29. A dice has six numbers on its sides, from 1 to 6. You can throw a dice and it will land on one of the sides with a number.

If you throw a dice many times, which sentence is likely to be correct?

- ○ It is more likely you will throw a six (6) than a one (1).
- ○ It is more likely you will throw a one (1) than a six (6).
- ○ A one (1) or a six (6) are equally likely.

30. A shop cuts some cakes into four different pieces or fractions.

The pieces are one-quarter, one-third, one-half and three-quarters. The different fractions or parts are shown below.

one-third   three-quarters   one-half   one-quarter

Bunt asks for two pieces that are the same size.

When the two pieces are added together, Bunt has more than half but less than a whole cake.

Which two pieces of cake did Bunt ask for?

one-quarter   one-half   three-quarters   one-third

○   ○   ○   ○

END OF TEST

How did you go with these test questions? Some were probably harder questions for you. There might have been some questions that you have not yet learnt in class but you can use these questions to help you learn. Check to see where you did well and where you had problems. Try to revise the questions that were hard for you.

Use the chart on pages 63–64 to see which level of performance you reached. Again we remind you that this is only an estimate. Don't be surprised if you answered some difficult questions correctly or even missed some easier questions.

There is now only one more Numeracy Test to practise. The last test contains 36 questions.

Instructions

- As you check the answer for each question, mark it as correct (✓) or incorrect (✗). Mark any questions that you omitted or left out as incorrect (✗) for the moment.
- Then look at how many questions you answered correctly in each level.
- You will be able to see what level you are at by finding the point where you started having consistent difficulty with questions at a certain level. For example, if you answered most questions correctly up to the Intermediate level and then got most questions wrong from then onwards, it is likely your ability is at the Intermediate level. You can ask your parents or your teacher to help you do this if it isn't clear to you.

Am I able to ...

	SKILL	ESTIMATED LEVEL	✓ or ✗
1	Recognise shapes in a figure?	Standard	
2	Write how many hundreds, tens and units there are in a number?	Standard	
3	Divide a two-digit number by two?	Standard	
4	Draw a line of set length?	Standard	
5	Write numbers which are more than and less than a specified number?	Standard	
6	Identify the time on a clockface?	Standard	
7	Divide an uneven quantity into three equal groups?	Standard	
8	Identify the net of a 3D shape?	Advanced	
9	Measure the liquid in a jug?	Intermediate	
10	Combine the amounts in a table?	Intermediate	
11	State the direction of travel?	Intermediate	
12	State the direction of travel?	Intermediate	
13	Divide a quantity into groups?	Intermediate	
14	Visualise the symmetry of a folded shape?	Intermediate	
15	Find a difference in length using subtraction?	Intermediate	
16	Multiply the cost of an article and then add another value?	Intermediate	
17	Recognise a number series decreasing by three?	Intermediate	
18	Interpret data in a simple chart?	Intermediate	
19	Match tiles to a design?	Intermediate	
20	Count the number of edges on a pyramid with some sides not visible?	Intermediate	
21	Recognise an image that has been flipped, turned or rotated?	Advanced	

	SKILL	ESTIMATED LEVEL	✓ or ✗
22	Record numbers in expanded notation?	Intermediate	
23	Interpret data from a table?	Intermediate	
24	Interpret data from a table?	Advanced	
25	Interpret data from a chart?	Advanced	
26	Select a mathematical operation to find an answer?	Advanced	
27	Define an even number?	Advanced	
28	Recognise the element of chance in daily activities?	Advanced	
29	Indicate the probability of an outcome?	Advanced	
30	Double a fraction to be more than a half but less than a whole?	Advanced	
	TOTAL		

This is the last Numeracy Test. This test has the exact same number of questions as the Year 3 NAPLAN Online Numeracy Test. There are 36 questions. There are six more questions than in Test 5.

If you aren't sure what to do, ask your teacher or your parents to help you. Don't be afraid to ask if it isn't clear to you.

Allow around 45 minutes for this test.

Write the answer in the box or colour in the circle with the correct answer. Colour in only one circle for each answer.

1. Which number below is the largest?
   ○ 34
   ○ 43
   ○ 41
   ○ 39

Did you colour in one of the circles?

2. Which is the tallest tree?

   ○   ○   ○   ○

3. Write one hundred and forty-nine as a number.

Write your answer in the box.

4. What is this object? Colour one of the circles for your answer.

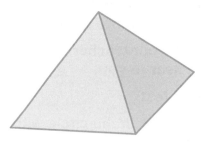

cylinder   pyramid   cube   parallelogram

○   ○   ○   ○

5. Which of the following objects is normally used to measure weight?

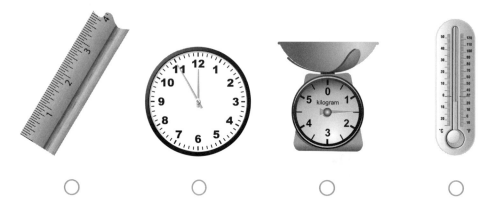

○   ○   ○   ○

6. Here are some coins.

Which coins would we use to make $1.75?

○ $2, 50c, 20c, 5c

○ $1, 50c, 20c, 5c

○ 50c, 20c, 10c, 5c

○ $1, 50c, 20c, 10c, 5c

7. Which object below is a hexagon?

○   ○   ○   ○

8. What is the answer to this sum?

$$25 + 7 = \boxed{}$$

Write your answer in the box.

9. How much milk is in this baby bottle?

○ 50 mL

○ 100 mL

○ 150 mL

○ 200 mL

10. Here are some stars.

If we gave away half of these stars, how many would we have left?

6   7   8   9

○   ○   ○   ○

11. Which of the watches below shows the time as half past ten?

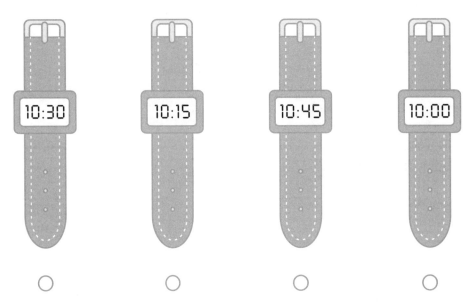

○   ○   ○   ○

12. Each dog below has eight (8) spots.

How would we work out how many spots there are in total?

    8 − 4   4 + 4 + 4 + 4   8 + 8 + 8 + 8

    ○   ○   ○

It would be a good idea to check your answers to questions 1 to 12 before moving on to the other questions.

☞ **Tip for Question 13**

Here are some numbers which are three less and three more than the number in the circle. This is an example:

Example

13 − ⬤16 + 19

13. Now write the numbers which are three less and three more than the number in the circle below.

☐ − ⬤38 + ☐

> **Write your answer in the boxes.**

Here is a calendar for a month of the year.

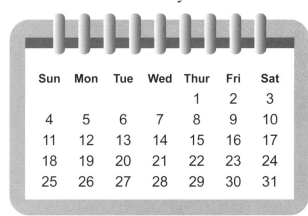

Sun	Mon	Tue	Wed	Thur	Fri	Sat
				1	2	3
4	5	6	7	8	9	10
11	12	13	14	15	16	17
18	19	20	21	22	23	24
25	26	27	28	29	30	31

> **Write your answer in the box.**

☐

14. What date is the second Wednesday on this calendar?

15. If we told you that this was the calendar for the month of April, what mistake is there in this calendar? Write your answer on the line.

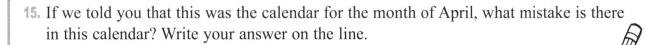

_____

_____

16. Look at the following chart.

The symbol ✸ is at D4.

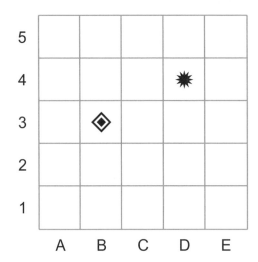

In what position is the symbol ◈?

A4	B3	A3	D4
○	○	○	○

---

17. Sean earns $5 for every sheep he shears.

If Sean shears five sheep, how much does he earn?

$20	$25	$30	$35
○	○	○	○

18. It took 18 minutes to iron some shirts. Each shirt took three minutes to iron.

How many shirts were ironed?

3	4	5	6
○	○	○	○

19. Here is a piece of wood that is 60 cm long. It is cut into pieces that are each 10 cm long.

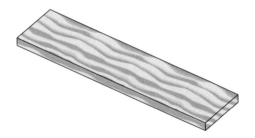

Which number sentence below will show how many pieces were cut?

10×60	$10 \div 60$	60×10	$60 \div 10$
○	○	○	○

20. Here is a pattern made up of coloured diamonds. The diamonds look like this with four sides.

How many coloured diamonds are needed to cover all the area in the grey shape?

12	10	9	6
○	○	○	○

21. There is a pattern in these five shapes.

Which should come next in this pattern?

    ◯   ◯   ◯   ◯

---

22. $29 + 13$ is the same as $30 + \boxed{?}$

> **Write your answer in the box.**

---

23. The table below shows how many cars Steve the mechanic serviced last week. The numbers are shown as tallies or marked lines.

Monday	⦀⦀ I
Tuesday	IIII
Wednesday	⦀⦀ III
Thursday	⦀⦀ ⦀⦀
Friday	⦀⦀ ⦀⦀
Saturday	⦀⦀ ⦀⦀ II

How many cars altogether did he service on Friday and Saturday?

    12   17   22   25

    ◯   ◯   ◯   ◯

24. Carta is packing drinks into boxes. Each box holds four drinks.

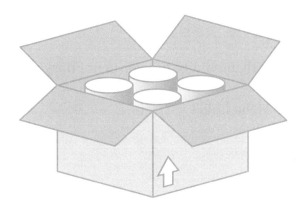

She has 22 drinks. How many boxes will she need to pack all the drinks?

4	5	6	7
○	○	○	○

It would be a good idea to check your answers to questions 13 to 24 before moving on to the other questions.

25. Here is a pattern of numbers:

32   26   20   14   ☐?☐

What is the next number in this pattern?

8	10	12	16
○	○	○	○

26. Here is a pattern of daisies. How many will be next?

   ?

Did you colour in one of the circles?

9	10	11	12
○	○	○	○

27. There are three children with balloons. They are Aira, Fouska and Helia.

- Aira has 12 balloons.
- Fouska has 18 balloons.
- Helia has more balloons than Aira but fewer than Fouska.

How many balloons does Helia hold?

○ more than 18

○ beween 12 and 18

○ about 6

○ less than 12

28. If we flipped this number sideways, this is what it would look like.

Flipped sideways (turned over)

What would this number look like if we flipped it sideways?

○   ○   ○   ○

29. We have $15. We would like to buy some apples for $3.50, some grapes for $5 and some bananas for $4.

How would we work out how much change we should receive from our $15?

○ $15 − $3.50 + $5 + $4

○ $15 − $3.50 − $5 − $4

○ ($3.50 + $5 + $4) − $15

30. $62 - 8 =$ [ ]

Write your answer in the box.

31. This is part of a bus timetable. It shows the time, the bus number and where the bus is going.

Time	Bus number	Destination
9:00 am	393	Central Railway
9:15 am	395	Central Railway
9:30 am	397	Circular Quay
9:45 am	399	Circular Quay
10:00 am	400	Bondi
10:15 am	M10	Leichhardt
10:30 am	394	Circular Quay
10:45 am	396	Circular Quay
11:00 am	M10	Leichhardt

If the time is 9:30 am, how long will I need to wait for a bus to Leichhardt?

15 minutes ○   30 minutes ○   45 minutes ○   60 minutes ○

32. Here is a table of numbers. There are five numbers on the left. The numbers on the right follow a special rule.

LEFT	RIGHT
8	40
10	50
12	60
15	75
20	100

What is the special rule for the numbers on the right?

○ They increase by 2.

○ They increase by 10.

○ They multiply the left number by 5.

☞ **Tip for Question 33**

There are signs missing in these sums. Use a $+$, $-$, $\times$ or $\div$ to fill the spaces. The spaces are shown with dots. Here is an example.

Example

$$6 \dots (3 \dots 1) = 3$$

The missing symbols are:

$$6 \div (3 - 1) = 6 \div 2 = 3$$

---

33. Insert two missing symbols between these numbers:

$$5 \dots 3 \dots 1 = 3$$

---

34. There are nine gold bars to be divided between two people. Aura will get twice as many as Inga.

How much will each person get?

Aura will get [ ] .

Inga will get [ ] .

Write your answer in the boxes.

---

35. Gisele cut a white shape out of the green paper. Then she folded the paper in half diagonally.

Fold down

Fold along the line

Which shape did Gisele see?

○　　　　○　　　　○　　　　○

36. This is what my puppy Rosie looks like on her first birthday.

Each year she develops more spots according to a secret pattern.

This is what my puppy Rosie looks like on her second birthday.

This is what my puppy Rosie looks like on her third birthday.

How many spots will Rosie have on her 10th birthday?

○ 10　　　○ 12　　　○ 14　　　○ 18

END OF TEST

Again you have done quite well if you managed to complete all of these tests. We tried to vary the questions and some were probably a little harder.

Check to see where you did well and where you had problems. Try to revise the questions that were hard for you. Then it is time for a rest.

Use the chart on pages 78–79 to see which level of performance you reached. Again we remind you that this is only an estimate. Don't be surprised if you answered some difficult questions correctly or even missed some easier questions.

Instructions

- As you check the answer for each question, mark it as correct (✓) or incorrect (✗). Mark any questions that you omitted or left out as incorrect (✗) for the moment.
- Then look at how many questions you answered correctly in each level.
- You will be able to see what level you are at by finding the point where you started having consistent difficulty with questions at a certain level. For example, if you answered most questions correctly up to the Intermediate level and then got most questions wrong from then onwards, it is likely your ability is at the Intermediate level. You can ask your parents or your teacher to help you do this if it isn't clear to you.

Am I able to ...

	SKILL	ESTIMATED LEVEL	✓ or ✗
1	Recognise the largest number?	Standard	
2	Select the tallest object?	Standard	
3	Write a three-digit number?	Standard	
4	Recognise a pyramid?	Standard	
5	Choose the object that is used to measure weight?	Standard	
6	Find a value in coins?	Standard	
7	Identify a hexagon?	Standard	
8	Complete a two-digit and one-digit addition?	Standard	
9	Measure the level of liquid at an intermediate level in a bottle?	Standard	
10	Find half of an illustrated quantity?	Standard	
11	Identify the time on a digital clock?	Standard	
12	State a simple addition equation to solve a problem?	Standard	
13	Increase and decrease a number by a given amount?	Standard	
14	Read the date on a calendar?	Standard	
15	Find an error in a calendar?	Intermediate	
16	Locate the position of an object on a grid?	Intermediate	
17	Multiply a quantity?	Intermediate	
18	Divide a quantity?	Intermediate	
19	Write a number statement for a division?	Intermediate	
20	Work out how many regular shapes fit into a larger figure?	Intermediate	
21	Complete a series of shapes with a regular order?	Intermediate	
22	Complete an equation?	Intermediate	
23	Read tally marks and add them?	Intermediate	

	SKILL	ESTIMATED LEVEL	✓ or ✗
24	Divide a quantity that has a remainder into groups?	Intermediate	
25	Complete a sequence reducing by six?	Intermediate	
26	Recognise a number sequence?	Advanced	
27	Describe a range for a value?	Advanced	
28	Flip a shape horizontally?	Advanced	
29	Indicate the correct number sentence to solve a problem?	Advanced	
30	Solve a subtraction?	Advanced	
31	Read from a timetable to find the time required to wait?	Advanced	
32	Find a numerical rule?	Advanced	
33	Insert mathematical operators?	Advanced	
34	Solve a problem with proportions?	Advanced	
35	Visualise a folded shape?	Advanced	
36	Work out the continuing number pattern and use this to solve a problem?	Advanced	
	TOTAL		

This is the first Reading Test. There are 10 questions.

If you aren't sure what to do, ask your teacher or your parents to help you. Don't be afraid to ask if it isn't clear to you.

Allow around 15 to 20 minutes for this test.

In this test you will need to look at a picture or read something first. Then read each question and colour in the circle with the correct answer. Sometimes you will instead have to write an answer in the space provided.

Here is a picture with two words.

1. Which word in the picture means 'joy'?

Happy ○   Birthday ○

Did you colour in one of the circles?

Read the poem and answer questions 2 to 6.

2. What could be the name of this poem?
   - ○ The beach
   - ○ Summer holiday
   - ○ Not growing old

3. What colour is the sky in the poem?
   - ○ white
   - ○ grey
   - ○ blue

4. What time of year is this vacation?
   - ○ summer
   - ○ autumn
   - ○ winter
   - ○ spring

5. What do the children in the poem want?
   - ○ to be on vacation
   - ○ to see the waves
   - ○ to be back at school

6. What is one thing that the children **do not** want?
   - ○ sandcastle made of gold
   - ○ to stay young
   - ○ to ever grow old
   - ○ to be free to explore

We love summer days

Where the sky is so blue,

When we walk to the beach

And our folks will come too.

We wait for vacations

To play all day long,

Being free to explore

Or just humming a song.

We can watch silver waves

Make a sandcastle made of gold,

So the last thing we want

Is to ever grow old.

Look at the docket from a store and answer questions 7 to 10.

IDLA SUPERMARKET
ABN 602 934 496 2

689 Cazna Parade
MAROUBRA JUNCTION NSW 2035

Served by NICK B

Docket No.	Date	Time
26862	27.9.10	2:30

Description	Cost
Yoghurt	$3.50
Bread	$3.20
Sultanas	$3.45
Peaches	$3.15
Tomatoes	$2.85
Frozen fish	$4.15
Cheese	$2.95
Eggs	$2.75
Rice	$3.05
Macaroni	$0.75
Total	$29.80
Cash	$40.00
Change:	
Cash	$10.20

SATISFACTION GUARANTEED

7. Which was the most expensive thing purchased?

cash   yoghurt   frozen fish
○   ○   ○

8. What was the total cost of all the items?
   ○ $29.80
   ○ $40.00
   ○ $22.20
   ○ $0.75

9. What is the address of the store? Write your answer on the line.

   _____

10. What type of store is this?
    ○ supermarket
    ○ fruit and vegetable shop
    ○ hardware store
    ○ department store

END OF TEST

Well done! You have completed the first Reading Test. This test had different types of questions. They were like comprehension passages. You had to look at something or read something and then make a judgement.

How did you find these questions? We hope you found them interesting. Revise anything that was hard for you. There are further questions in the next Reading Test. The next test contains some different questions. Take a long break before doing any more tests.

Use the diagnostic chart on page 84 to see which level of ability you reached. This is only an estimate. Don't be surprised if you answered some difficult questions correctly or even missed some easier questions.

Please note that multiple interpretations are possible for the levels of difficulty of these tasks. Also some questions involve skills from different levels. This Is only an initial guide to the approximate level of the reading skill assessed.

Instructions

- As you check the answer for each question, mark it as correct (✓) or incorrect (✗).
- Mark any questions that you missed or left out as incorrect (✗) for the moment.
- Go back and practise the questions you missed out or got incorrect. You can ask your parents or your teacher to help you do this if it isn't clear to you.
- For this first Reading test we have given you only one question higher than Standard level to begin with.

Am I able to ...

	SKILL	ESTIMATED LEVEL	✓ or ✗
1	Find the meaning of a word in a picture?	Standard	
2	Find the title of a poem?	Standard	
3	Locate a fact in a short poem?	Standard	
4	Locate a fact in a short poem?	Standard	
5	Interpret the meaning of some words?	Intermediate	
6	Find clearly stated information?	Standard	
7	Find clearly stated information?	Standard	
8	Make connections between pieces of clearly stated information?	Standard	
9	Find clearly stated information?	Standard	
10	Make connections between pieces of clearly stated information?	Standard	
	TOTAL		

This is the second Reading Test. There are 15 questions.

If you aren't sure what to do, ask your teacher or your parents to help you. Don't be afraid to ask if it isn't clear to you.

Allow around 20 to 25 minutes for this test.

In this test you will need to look at a picture or read something first. Then read each question and colour in the circle with the correct answer. Sometimes you will instead have to write an answer in the space provided.

Here is a picture of some money.

1. How much is this money?

   ○ one dollar

   ○ five dollars

   ○ twenty dollars

   ○ 550 266 dollars

2. From which country did this money come?

   ○ Australia

   ○ New Zealand

   ○ United Kingdom

Did you colour in one of the circles?

Here are four pictures that tell a story.

3   What is the story about?

○ people at the movies

○ how TV actors work

○ how a movie is made

Did you colour in one of the circles?

Read the poem and answer questions 4 to 8.

Rain

By Robert Louis Stevenson

The rain is raining all around,

It falls on field and tree,

It rains on the umbrellas here,

And on the ships at sea.

From the Project Gutenberg e-book of *A Child's Garden of Verses* by Robert Louis Stevenson, Charles Scribner's Sons, New York, 1905, p. 9

4. What is the name of this poem?

○ Robert Louis Stevenson

○ The rain is raining all around

○ Rain

5. Who wrote this poem?

   ○ Rain

   ○ Robert Louis Stevenson

   ○ Umbrella

6. Which word rhymes with *tree*?

   ○ around

   ○ here

   ○ sea

   ○ rain

7. This poem tells us some places where the rain fell. Where did the rain fall?

   ○ down the drains

   ○ in the dams and ponds

   ○ on the raincoats

   ○ on the umbrellas

8. Look at these pictures of two book covers. In which book do you think you would find the poem on page 86?

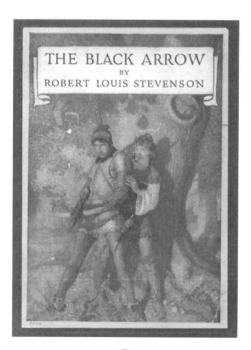

○   ○

Sources: The Project Gutenberg e-book of *A Child's Garden of Verses* by Robert Louis Stevenson

The Project Gutenberg e-book of *The Black Arrow* by Robert Louis Stevenson

Read *Why is the sky so blue?* and answer questions 9 to 12.

Why is the sky so blue?

It was a sunny day. Michaela asked her mother, 'Why is the sky so blue?'

Her mother said, 'Our light comes from the sun. Did you know that it travels all that way? Michaela, this light looks white but it is really a mixture of the colours of the rainbow.'

'Do you mean violet, indigo, green, blue, yellow, orange and red?' said Michaela.

'Yes', said her mother. 'When these colours come from the sun they travel through the air around our planet. There are many tiny parts of this air that we cannot see,' she added.

'Well, Michaela, what happens is this. The light changes when it hits these tiny parts. Most of the colours are taken up by these parts of the air but the blue light is not. The blue light is then reflected, like in a mirror.'

9. What is the name of the girl who is talking to her mother?
Write your answer on the line.

_____

10. What do we learn about the light from the sun?

○ The light from the sun is the colour of a rainbow.

○ The light from the sun is yellow.

○ The light from the sun is white.

11. What makes the light change colour?

- ○ the violet, indigo, green, blue, yellow, orange and red light
- ○ the tiny parts of the air that we cannot see
- ○ the light from the rainbow

12. Which colour is **not** taken up by the tiny parts of the air?
(Colour in only one of the circles.)

- ○ white   ○ violet
- ○ indigo   ○ green
- ○ blue   ○ yellow
- ○ orange   ○ red

Did you colour in one of the circles?

Read *The good friend* and answer questions 13 to 15.

The good friend

Jim was riding his bike home after school. He was pushed off his bike and robbed. The robbers took everything that was his and left Jim by the roadside.

An older boy from the same school walked down that road but when he saw Jim he went right around him. Then a man drove by and when he saw what had happened he just hurried past.

But a young boy from another school was also travelling home on his bike. When he saw Jim lying by the side of the road he felt very sorry for Jim. He stopped. He went over to Jim. He gave Jim some water and put a bandage on his arm.

Then he helped Jim onto his own bike and wheeled him to the hospital. He asked the nurses to look after Jim. He told them what had happened.

The next day he visited Jim in hospital. They became good friends.

13. What happened to Jim?

○ He was riding his bike home from school and was robbed.

○ He was walking home from school when he was robbed.

○ He was riding his bike to school and was robbed.

14. Who helped Jim?

○ an older boy from the same school

○ a young boy from another school

○ a man who drove by

15. Where did the young boy take Jim?

○ school

○ home

○ police station

○ hospital

Did you colour in one of the circles?

END OF TEST

Well done! You have completed the second Reading Test.

How did you find these questions? We hope you found them interesting. Revise anything that was hard for you. The next test contains some different questions. Now take a long break before doing any more tests.

Use the diagnostic chart on page 91 to see which level of ability you reached. This is only an estimate. Don't be surprised if you answered some difficult questions correctly or even missed some easier questions.

Please note that multiple interpretations are possible for the levels of difficulty of these tasks. Also some questions involve skills from different levels. This is only an initial guide to the approximate level of the reading skill assessed.

Instructions

- As you check the answer for each question, mark it as correct (✓) or incorrect (✗). Mark any questions that you omitted or left out as incorrect (✗) for the moment.
- Then look at how many questions you answered correctly in each level.
- You will be able to see what level you are at by finding the point where you started having consistent difficulty with questions at a certain level. For example, if you answered most questions correctly up to the Intermediate level and then got most questions wrong from then onwards, it is likely your ability is at the Intermediate level. You can ask your parents or your teacher to help you do this if it isn't clear to you.

Am I able to ...

	SKILL	ESTIMATED LEVEL	✓ or ✗
1	Identify the value of currency from an image?	Standard	
2	Find clearly stated information?	Standard	
3	Make some meaning from images in a sequence?	Standard	
4	Find the name of a poem?	Standard	
5	Find the author of a poem?	Standard	
6	Identify a rhyming word?	Intermediate	
7	Find clearly stated information?	Standard	
8	Relate a poem to a book of verse?	Standard	
9	Write the name of a character?	Standard	
10	Make connections between pieces of clearly stated information?	Intermediate	
11	State the cause of an event?	Intermediate	
12	Exclude a factor from a list?	Intermediate	
13	Find a clearly stated detail?	Standard	
14	Make a connection to a person in the story?	Standard	
15	Find an outcome?	Standard	
	TOTAL		

This is the third Reading Test. There are 20 questions.

If you aren't sure what to do, ask your teacher or your parents to help you. Don't be afraid to ask if it isn't clear to you.

Allow around 25 to 30 minutes for this test.

In this test you will need to look at a picture or read something first. Then read each question and colour in the circle with the correct answer. Sometimes you will instead have to write an answer in the space provided.

Look at this picture and answer questions 1 to 4.

Be sure to visit

Children's Art Display
Paintings Sculptures Prints

Central Library
4–14 June 2011

1. What is this picture?

   ○ It is a sign asking people to see children's art.

   ○ It is a sign asking people to come and paint.

   ○ It is a sign asking people to buy paintings.

   ○ It is a sign asking people to borrow books from the library.

Did you colour in one of the circles?

2. What is one thing that the children will show?

their library	their music	their sculptures	their books
○	○	○	○

3. What is a *display*?

a show	a sale	a concert	reading
○	○	○	○

4. Where will the children's art display take place?

Children's Art Display	Art Gallery	Central Library
○	○	○

Read *Maria* and answer questions 5 to 8.

Maria

Maria is eight years old. She came to town last month. Maria lives in the new house near the park. She lives with her parents and two brothers.

Maria likes her school. She is making friends. Her favourite subject is reading. The teacher thinks Maria can read very well.

Maria likes to help around the house. Her mother says that she will be a good cook.

On Fridays Maria plays netball at school. She also plays soccer every Saturday. Maria has scored many goals. She is a good soccer player. Maria wants to play for Australia.

Maria asks her friends over on Sunday afternoon. They listen to music or watch a DVD.

5. How many people are there in Maria's family?

three	four	five	six
○	○	○	○

6. What is Maria's favourite subject at school?

    netball   soccer   music   reading   cooking

    ○   ○   ○   ○   ○

7. What does Maria do on a Saturday?

    plays netball   plays soccer   plays music   reads

    ○   ○   ○   ○

8. What would Maria like to do one day?

  ○ She would like to be a good cook.

  ○ She would like to listen to music or watch a video.

  ○ She would like to play for the Australian women's soccer team.

  ○ She would like to invite some friends over.

Look at this sign and answer questions 9 to 12.

Source: http://commons.wikimedia.org/wiki/File:Wee_Willie_Winkie_1940_poster.jpg

9. Where is Wee Willie Winkie running in this poster?

○ through the town   ○ through the library   ○ through the school

10. What is he wearing?

○ a tracksuit

○ a nightgown

○ a long shirt

○ a dressing gown

11. What will Wee Willie Winkie count?

○ the number of upstairs

○ the number of downstairs

○ the number of windows

○ the number of nooks

○ the number of children reading library books

12. What word in the sign rhymes with, or has the same sound as, *town*?

○ gowns

○ books

○ gown

○ nooks

○ count

Read *How to make some biscuits* and answer questions 13 to 16.

How to make some biscuits

This is a recipe for oatmeal cookies. It takes around 15 minutes to prepare and around 12 minutes to cook. You will need a parent or other adult to supervise. Do not try this by yourself.

Ingredients:

1 cup quick cooking oats

½ cup wholemeal self-raising flour

1 tablespoon brown sugar

1 tablespoon butter

1 teaspoon vanilla extract

½ teaspoon ground cinnamon

boiling water

Directions:

1. Combine everything and mix well.
2. Mix in boiling water (ask a parent to do this) until it becomes firm.
3. Press, rub and squeeze this mixture.
4. Roll it out to ½ cm thickness—use a board dusted with some flour to make it easier.
5. Cut the dough into shapes.
6. Place the shapes on baking trays—use non-stick baking trays.
7. Bake in the oven (160 °C) for around 12 minutes (ask a parent to do this).
8. Remove from the oven (ask a parent to do this).
9. Allow the biscuits to cool.

13. What is included in a recipe?

○ ingredients and directions for cooking

○ evidence that you have paid for a meal

○ the way to serve some food

14. Why is it necessary to ask a parent or adult for help?

○ Some things are too heavy to carry.

○ Some things are too hot to touch.

○ Some things are too complicated to do by yourself.

15. Which is more: a teaspoon or a tablespoon?

teaspoon   tablespoon

○   ○

16. How much flour is needed?

one cup ○   half a cup ○   a tablespoon ○

Read this passage and answer questions 17 to 20.

Once upon a time a man owned a wonderful goose. Every day it laid a golden egg.

The man sold the eggs. Soon he became rich. But he was impatient. The goose gave him only one golden egg a day. He wanted to get rich quicker.

Then one day he had an idea. He would get all the golden eggs at once. He would kill the goose and cut it open. He did not find even one golden egg and now his precious goose was dead.

Source: http://www.gutenberg.org/files/19994/19994-h/images/i063.jpg

17. What is the meaning of this story? Colour in only one circle. The meaning of the story is that

○ you should look after your pets.

○ geese only lay eggs for nice people.

○ if you have plenty and you want even more you might lose everything.

18. What is a good title for this story?

○ The Goose and the Golden Egg

○ The Golden Goose

○ The Golden Egg

○ The Farmer and the Golden Egg

19. What is another word or phrase for *impatient*?

○ sick

○ in a hurry

○ worried

○ tolerant

20. What mistake did the man make?

○ He thought that the goose was greedy and laid only one egg a day.

○ He thought that the goose had all the golden eggs inside her.

○ He thought that he could take out many golden eggs but the goose would still lay some more for him.

○ He was worried that the goose might stop laying golden eggs.

END OF TEST

Well done! You have completed the third Reading Test.

How did you find these questions? We hope that you found them interesting. Revise anything that was hard for you. The next test contains some different questions. Now take a long break before doing any more tests.

Use the diagnostic chart on page 99 to see which level of ability you reached. This is only an estimate. Don't be surprised if you answered some difficult questions correctly or even missed some easier questions.

Please note that multiple interpretations are possible for the levels of difficulty of these tasks. Also some questions involve skills from different levels. This is only an initial guide to the approximate level of the reading skill assessed.

Instructions

- As you check the answer for each question, mark it as correct (✓) or incorrect (✗). Mark any questions that you omitted or left out as incorrect (✗) for the moment.

- Then look at how many questions you answered correctly in each level.

- You will be able to see what level you are at by finding the point where you started having consistent difficulty with questions at a certain level. For example, if you answered most questions correctly up to the Intermediate level and then got most questions wrong from then onwards, it is likely your ability is at the Intermediate level. You can ask your parents or your teacher to help you do this if it isn't clear to you.

Am I able to ...

	SKILL	ESTIMATED LEVEL	✓ or ✗
1	Understand the message of a poster or sign?	Standard	
2	Find clearly stated information?	Standard	
3	Define a word from a poster?	Intermediate	
4	State the location of an event listed on a poster?	Standard	
5	Determine the characters in a story?	Standard	
6	Find information in a passage?	Standard	
7	Find information in a passage?	Standard	
8	State the intention of a person in the story?	Intermediate	
9	Find the location of an action in a simple verse?	Standard	
10	Find information in a passage?	Standard	
11	Find a detailed fact in a verse?	Intermediate	
12	Locate a word that rhymes?	Intermediate	
13	Recognise a common meaning?	Intermediate	
14	Understand the reason for a caution?	Intermediate	
15	Distinguish between two quantities?	Standard	
16	Find a fact in a recipe?	Standard	
17	Tell the meaning of a story?	Intermediate	
18	Give the name to a story?	Intermediate	
19	Find the meaning of a word?	Intermediate	
20	Discover the misconception of a character?	Intermediate	
	TOTAL		

An important note about the NAPLAN Online tests

The NAPLAN Online Reading test will be divided into different sections. Students will only have one opportunity to check their answers at the end of each section before proceeding to the next one. This means that after students have completed a section and moved onto the next they will not be able to check their work again. We have included reminders for students to check their work at specific points in the practice tests from now on so they become familiar with this process.

This is the fourth Reading Test. There are 25 questions.

If you aren't sure what to do, ask your teacher or your parents to help you. Don't be afraid to ask if it isn't clear to you.

Allow around 30 to 35 minutes for this test.

In this test you will need to look at a picture or read something first. Then read each question and colour in the circle with the correct answer. Sometimes you will instead have to write an answer in the space provided.

Look at the three book covers and answer questions 1 and 2.

1. Which one is *The Black Robe*?

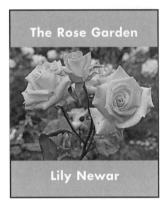

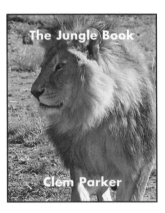

A	B	C
○	○	○

2. Which book was written by Lily Newar?

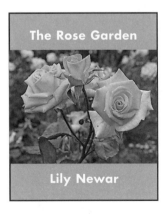

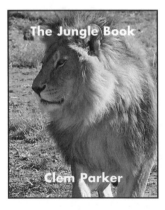

A	B	C
○	○	○

Read the passage and answer questions 3 to 7.

Adapted from *Summer Sandwiches*: http://thestir.cafemom.com/toddler/106597/toddler_meal_summer_sandwiches

Betty brings her lunch to school. She likes to decorate her sandwich.

Betty tells her friend Joanne, 'I put a funny face on my sandwich. It helps me to like food.'

She said, 'It is easy to make funny-face sandwiches. You just use colourful ingredients.' Betty uses olives, tomatoes, cucumbers, cheese or meat.

She wants Joanne to make funny-face sandwiches too. She told her friend, 'You can put a funny or sad or scary face on your sandwich. It is really fun.'

3. What is a good name or title for this passage?
   ○ School sandwiches
   ○ Funny faces
   ○ How to make a sandwich with a face
   ○ Funny-face sandwiches

4. Who made a funny-face sandwich?
   ○ Betty
   ○ Joanne
   ○ Betty's mother

5. What is Betty trying to do in this story?

○ She is trying to be a good sandwich maker.

○ She wants to see sandwiches with funny faces.

○ She is trying to convince Joanne to make funny-face sandwiches.

○ She is telling us how to make funny-face sandwiches.

6. What is the main meaning of this story?

○ A sandwich has colourful ingredients.

○ Children should make their sandwiches.

○ A sandwich does not need to be boring.

7. What is an *ingredient*?

a colour	a face	a part
○	○	○

Here are four pictures from a cartoon. The pictures tell a story.

Source: Wikimedia Commons, http://commons.wikimedia.org/wiki/File:Buster_Brown_-_It_probably_was_good_for_the_lad!.jpg

Look at the pictures and answer questions 8 and 9.

8. Who said 'Now, nice little boy. We will talk things over quietly'?

    the boy   the girl   the man

    ○   ○   ○

Did you colour in one of the circles?

9. Did the man talk things over quietly?

    yes   no

    ○   ○

Read *How to play a game* and answer questions 10 to 16.

How to play a game

Hide-and-seek is a game. You can play with only a few children or with many children.

First, choose a spot and call it 'home'. The home spot can be a wall or a post. Everyone has to agree just how far away they can hide. It should not be too close or too far away.

One person has to be 'in'. They close their eyes and then count to 20.

While this person is counting everyone else runs away to find a hiding place. When the person who is 'in' has finished counting to 20 they shout, 'Coming, ready or not!'

The person who is 'in' has to spot the other children and touch them before they make it to the home spot.

The person who is 'in' has to be careful. They need to guard the home spot but also wander around and look for the others. It is not easy sometimes.

The other players will try to run home when it is safe. If someone runs to home base without being touched, then he or she is safe.

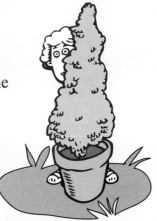

If you are 'in' and you see someone, you call their name and try to touch them before they can make it home. If you touch them, they are out of the game.

The game continues until all the children are found. The first person who is caught is 'in' for the next game.

10. Write the name of the game on the line. Write your answer on the line.

_____

11. What type of game is this?
- ○ It is a game that you play by yourself.
- ○ It is a game that you play with one other person.
- ○ It is a game that you play with other children.

12. When is someone safe?
- ○ They are safe when they are hiding.
- ○ They are safe if they run home without being touched.
- ○ They are safe when they wander around.
- ○ They are safe if they are touched when they run home.

13. Which person is 'in' for the next game?
- ○ the person who is hiding
- ○ the first person who runs home without being touched
- ○ the last person who is touched when they run home
- ○ the first person who is touched when they run home

14. Is it possible to be 'in' twice in a row in this game?
- ○ Yes, it is possible to be 'in' if everyone else is safe.
- ○ No, it is not possible because people take turns to be 'in'.

15. Write the numbers 1 to 6 in the boxes to show the order of the steps to play the game. The first one (1) has been done for you.

1	Choose a spot and call it 'home'.
	The first caught is 'in' for the next game.
	The counter shouts, 'Coming, ready or not!'
	The person 'in' spots other children and touches them before they make it home.
	One person has to be 'in'. They close their eyes and count to 20.
	While the counter is counting, everyone runs away to hide.

16. When is the game finished?

○ The game is finished only when everyone is safe.

○ The game is finished when you count to 20.

○ The game is finished when the first person is touched while running to home.

○ The game is finished when the last person is touched or makes it home safe.

It would be a good idea to check your answers to questions 1 to 16 before moving on to the other questions.

Read *Koalas* and answer questions 17 to 20.

Koalas

The Australian koala is popular. It is often called a *koala bear*.

It is a furry animal that lives in a tree. It is grey and brown in colour. It can weigh about 5 to 14 kilograms.

The word *koala* comes from an Aboriginal word *gula*. Some say that it means 'no water'. Koalas can survive just by eating the leaves of gum trees. They eat around 500 grams of leaves each day. Koalas are herbivorous which means that they eat plants.

Koalas live in groups. They have their own home area. They are active at night and sleep for many hours each day so that they do not use up much energy.

Koalas are marsupials. This means that they raise their young in a pouch for around six months. A baby koala is only about 2 centimetres long. It weighs less than a gram. The young koalas are called *joeys*.

Koalas are found in Queensland, New South Wales, Victoria and South Australia. There are about 100 000 koalas left in the wild.

17. Which of the following points describe a koala? You can colour in more than one circle.

○ A baby koala eats 500 leaves a day.   ○ Koalas eat gum leaves.

○ Koalas are brown and grey in colour.   ○ A fully grown koala weighs 1 gram.

○ Koalas are carnivores.   ○ Koalas are furry animals.

18. Which of the following describe how a koala lives? Colour in three circles.

○ Koalas live in trees.   ○ Koalas live alone.

○ Koalas are herbivores.   ○ Koalas live in nests.

○ Koalas sleep at night.   ○ Koalas are marsupials.

19. Here is a map of Australia. Colour in the states where koalas still live.

20. Colour in the circles of the sentences that are true. You can colour in more than one circle for this question.

○ Koalas are bears.

○ *Joey* is an Aboriginal word for koala.

○ Koalas are meat-eaters.

○ *Gula* is an Aboriginal word for koala.

○ Herbivores are meat-eaters.

○ Koalas are furry.

○ Koalas eat leaves.

○ A baby koala stays in its mother's pouch.

Read *The golden fish* and answer questions 21 to 25.

The golden fish

This is a story about a young boy who lived in a town called Annam. His name was John and he was 12 years old.

Everyone liked John. They all said that he was an honest, hardworking boy. He tried to help his mother and look after his sister. They were very poor and often did not have enough food to eat.

After school, he would work at the shops. He was always smiling and friendly, even though he had many problems.

One day his little sister was very hungry and she was crying because there was no food. John loved his sister very much. He decided to help her even though he wanted to go to the park and play with his friends.

John asked his mother if he could go fishing at the local river. He wanted to bring home some food for his sister. It was only about 10 minutes from where he lived.

John sat by the edge of the water in the shade of a large willow tree. This was his favourite spot. He had been fishing there many times. The hours were passing but John was not having much luck. He started thinking about all the fun he missed out on by not going to the park. He felt sad but thought, 'I must never give in.'

Almost at once he felt a strong pull on the fishing line. It was a very large golden-red fish. John had never seen one like that before.

He dragged it ashore and ran home to his mother and sister, saying, 'Mum, Anna, look!' They ran outside to greet him and were all smiling. There would be plenty of food that night. But this is not the end of our story.

When his mother went to clean the fish, there was a huge surprise. Inside its belly she found a gold coin. No one could tell how it had got there but everyone was happy. They had food to eat and money to spare. John could not believe his good luck that day. He was really pleased that he had not gone to the park.

21. Why did people like John?

○ He worked after school at the shops.

○ He worked on the nearby farms.

○ He was honest.

○ He had many friends.

22. Why did John go fishing?

○ He did not want to play at the park.

○ He wanted to help his family.

○ He wanted to relax.

○ He wanted to find a coin.

Did you colour in one of the circles?

23. What does this story show about John?

○ He did not give up easily.

○ He was a strong boy when he pulled on the fishing line.

○ He had plenty of food.

24. This story is about a boy who

○ helps his family.

○ is helped by a farmer.

○ does not like to help.

○ likes to go to the park.

25. Which word in the story means luck?

fortune   smiling   gold

○   ○   ○

END OF TEST

Well done! You have completed the fourth Reading Test.

How did you find these questions? We hope you found them interesting. Revise anything that was hard for you. The next test contains some different questions. Now take a long break before doing any more tests.

Use the diagnostic chart on page 109 to see which level of ability you reached. This is only an estimate. Don't be surprised if you answered some difficult questions correctly or even missed some easier questions.

Please note that multiple interpretations are possible for the levels of difficulty of these tasks. Also some questions involve skills from different levels. This is only an initial guide to the approximate level of the reading skill assessed.

Instructions

- As you check the answer for each question, mark it as correct (✓) or incorrect (✗). Mark any questions that you omitted or left out as incorrect (✗) for the moment.
- Then look at how many questions you answered correctly in each level.
- You will be able to see what level you are at by finding the point where you started having consistent difficulty with questions at a certain level. For example, if you answered most questions correctly up to the Intermediate level and then got most questions wrong from then onwards, it is likely your ability is at the Intermediate level. You can ask your parents or your teacher to help you do this if it isn't clear to you.

Am I able to ...

	SKILL	ESTIMATED LEVEL	✓ or ✗
1	Read the title of a book?	Standard	
2	Read the name of the author of a book?	Standard	
3	Give a title to a passage?	Standard	
4	Identify a person in a passage?	Standard	
5	Identify a person's purpose?	Intermediate	
6	Find the main meaning in a story?	Intermediate	
7	Define a word?	Intermediate	
8	Indicate who is speaking in a cartoon?	Standard	
9	Contrast a word with an opposite action?	Advanced	
10	Write the name of the topic?	Intermediate	
11	State a requirement for a game?	Intermediate	
12	Understand a rule of the game?	Intermediate	
13	Understand a clearly stated rule of the game?	Intermediate	
14	Make connection from the passage to a potential outcome?	Advanced	
15	Order the steps to playing the game hide-and-seek?	Advanced	
16	State the condition for completing a game?	Intermediate	
17	Describe three features of an animal?	Intermediate	
18	Describe three aspects of an animal's behaviour?	Intermediate	
19	Connect verbal details to a map?	Intermediate	
20	Check the truth or falsity of claims?	Intermediate	
21	State the character of a person in a story?	Intermediate	
22	Find the reason for an action?	Intermediate	
23	Choose a key aspect of the character of a person in a story?	Intermediate	
24	Decide on the main message of the story?	Intermediate	
25	Find a word in the passage with a specific meaning?	Intermediate	
	TOTAL		

This is the fifth Reading Test. There are 30 questions.

If you aren't sure what to do, ask your teacher or your parents to help you. Don't be afraid to ask if it isn't clear to you.

Allow around 30 to 35 minutes for this test.

In this test you will need to look at a picture or read something first. Then read each question and colour in the circle with the correct answer. Sometimes you will instead have to write an answer in the space provided.

Read *Singapore* and answer questions 1 to 5.

Singapore

Anthony went to Singapore. He went with his family.

Chinese, Malays and Indians live there. The people live in tall apartment buildings.

It is a busy city. Tourists go there for shopping. You can buy almost anything in Singapore. There are many shopping centres.

The island is beautiful. There are many activities for visitors. One day Anthony's family caught a taxi. The driver was friendly. He told them that Singapore was once a small port. It was called *Temasek*. This means 'sea town'.

Anthony saw many interesting sights. There are gardens and a zoo. He went on a cable car. He caught a ferry to the island of Sentosa. It is nearby.

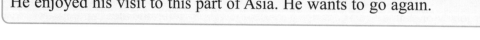

He enjoyed his visit to this part of Asia. He wants to go again.

1. What is the name of the city that Anthony visited?

   ○ China

   ○ Singapore

   ○ Temasek

   ○ Asia

2. Singapore was once a
   ○ shopping centre.
   ○ tall apartment building.
   ○ tourist centre.
   ○ small port.

3. Where do the people live?

   in apartments   in skyscrapers   in houses
        ○   ○   ○

4. What would Anthony like to do one day?
   ○ He would like to go to Temasek again.
   ○ He would like to go to Sentosa again.
   ○ He would like to go to Singapore again.
   ○ He would like to go on a cable car again.

5. Which word means 'sea town'?

   Singapore   Sentosa   Temasek
       ○   ○   ○

Look at this page from a book and answer questions 6 to 10.

GULLIVER'S TRAVELS INTO SEVERAL REMOTE NATIONS OF THE WORLD

BY JONATHAN SWIFT

DEAN OF ST. PATRICK'S, DUBLIN.

[First published in 1726]

From the Project Gutenberg e-book of *Gulliver's Travels* by Jonathan Swift, edited by Thomas M Balliet

6. What is this page?

   ○ the contents page   ○ the index   ○ the title page

7. Who is the author of this book?

   ○ Jonathan Swift   ○ St. Patrick   ○ Gulliver's travels

8. What is the best way to describe this book?

   ○ It is a book about a country.

   ○ It is a book about someone's adventures.

   ○ It is a book about someone's vacation.

9. What is the meaning of *remote* in this page from a book?

   ○ something that controls the TV

   ○ something that is nearby

   ○ something that is far away

   ○ something that is strange

10. In what way are *journey* and *travel* the same?

   ○ They are both a trip that someone makes.

   ○ They both use a plane to fly somewhere.

   ○ They are both vacations or holidays.

   ○ They both involve long distances.

It would be a good idea to check your answers to questions 1 to 10 before moving on to the other questions.

Read the passage and answer questions 11 to 20.

Jason is nine years old. He is tall for his age. He is lean, with short brown hair. He lives with his family in a red-brick house. They are close to the sea. The house is surrounded by a large garden. There are many shrubs, flowers and trees.

Every morning he likes to sit on the back veranda of his house. He tries to get up early each morning. If his father or mother is already awake, he says 'Good morning'.

Then he goes outside for a few minutes. Without trying to disturb anyone he tiptoes to the back door and unlocks it.

He sits on the white chair. This is under the striped awning that shades the veranda. He stares at the beauty of the new day. He looks at the golden sunrise. He sees clouds drifting in the sky.

Far away to the north, he can see the planes coming in to land at the nearby airport. He looks at the different types of jets with the help of binoculars. The planes glide gracefully in the sky. They remind him of giant pelicans that swoop down to the water.

Jason looks out past the hedge to a world far beyond. There are tall shrubs that surround the fence on all sides. He imagines that they are like giant soldiers on guard. These shrubs are called lilly pillies. They are filled with white flowers and red berries at this time of year.

He also hears the water gurgling from the fountain in the bird pond. It reminds him of being on holidays, when he would sit by the river bank and listen to the water bubbling over the rocks.

He likes this time of day. It is quiet and fresh. The birds are chirping in the trees. They fill the morning with their songs. Sometimes he brings a few slices of bread for them to eat and he enjoys watching them scramble for the crumbs. There are finches, rosellas and some honeyeaters at this time of year.

He loves to sit on the veranda. He likes to spend these few minutes by himself. Then it is time to do his many chores for the day.

11. What is the best name for this story?

○ Sitting on the veranda

○ The birds are chirping in the trees

○ Time to do his chores

○ The adventures of Jason

12. Is the name of the author of this passage shown?

      yes   no

      ○   ○

13. Which word rhymes with *lean*?

    send   men   been   lame

    ○   ○   ○   ○

14. Where is the main scene for the events in this story?

○ a red-brick house not far from the seaside

○ the back veranda of a house

○ a large garden with many shrubs, flowers and trees

○ the northern horizon

15. What is the meaning of the word *veranda* in the story?

   garden   backyard   porch   awning

   ○   ○   ○   ○

16. The planes remind Jason of which bird?

   finch   rosella   honeyeater   pelican

   ○   ○   ○   ○

17. What is the name of the shrubs that surround the fence?
Write your answer on the line.

_____

18. Colour in the circles next to those things that Jason can see from his veranda. You can colour in more than one circle.

○ his family   ○ the pelicans

○ the seaside   ○ the giant soldiers

○ the airport   ○ the water gurgling

○ the awning   ○ the sunrise

19. Which picture shows binoculars?

○   ○   ○

20. After reading this story, how could we describe Jason?

○ He is a polite boy.

○ He likes to rest in the morning before starting his work.

○ He likes the peace of the morning.

○ He does not have any friends.

It would be a good idea to check your answers to questions 11 to 20 before moving on to the other questions.

Read *Facts about emus* and answer questions 21 to 24.

Facts about emus

The word emu comes from the Portuguese word *ema*.

The emu is found only in Australia.

The emu is a large flightless bird.

Emus live all over Australia, mainly in grasslands.

Emus have long strong legs for running.

Emus reach up to 2 metres in height.

Female emus are generally larger than the males.

Emu feathers are grey-brown.

Emus have long necks that are bluish-black.

Emus have long legs which allow them to run very fast.

Emus can sprint at 50 kilometres per hour.

Emus make grunting noises and also a deep drumming sound.

Emus are omnivorous, meaning they eat both plants and meat.

Emus generally find partners in summer and breed in the winter months, May to August.

Male emus incubate and raise the young.

Emus can live between 10 and 20 years in the wild.

21. Colour in the circles next to the statements that are true.
You can colour in more than one circle.

○ Emus are birds but they can't fly.

○ Emus eat grass, seeds and insects.

○ Emus are the largest birds in the world.

○ Emu eggs are cared for by the mother.

22. The emu is shown on the Australian coat of arms. Which one of the following is the Australian coat of arms?

○   ○   ○

23. How fast can emus run?

2 km per hour   10–20 km per hour   50 km per hour
○   ○   ○

24. Which word means 'keep warm'?

flightless   omnivorous   incubate
○   ○   ○

Read *Blind man's bluff* and answer questions 25 and 26.

Blind man's buff

When the coldest wind is howling,
And my friends come over to play,
Then we gather by the fire that's glowing,
To enjoy the winter's day.

We always start with Blind-man's Buff
Our favourite now for years—
It's the game that really makes us laugh,
That fills the room with shouts and cheers

Source: Wikimedia Commons

25. What is this poem about?

○ things to do to keep warm

○ the game that we enjoy most of all

○ how to keep a fire glowing

○ how to make people laugh

26. For what season was the poem written?

summer	spring	autumn	winter
○	○	○	○

Read *On the front porch* and answer questions 27 to 30.

On the front porch

It was late afternoon. John was sitting with his mother, Mrs Ford, and his sister Anna on the front porch. At that time of day it was much cooler outside.

The sun was now setting over the mountains. The sky was a mixture of orange and purple. It was very beautiful.

There was stillness in the air. Flocks of birds were flying home to their nests. Peacefulness had settled over the countryside. The three of them were talking.

John noticed a speck on the road that led into town. As time passed the speck grew larger. He could see the outline of a man. He was walking towards their home.

His mother and sister were a little startled. It was unusual for strangers to be walking along the main road, let alone towards their house, especially at that time of day.

The man approached the front gate. He was tall, lean and well dressed. He wore a coat and tie. His gold-rimmed spectacles were perched on the tip of his nose. He looked a little tired from his walking. The man apologised for troubling them. He introduced himself.

He said that he was a doctor, Dr Goodman, from the hospital in the neighbouring city. He was on his way into town when all of a sudden his car stopped by the roadside. He could not start the car and was unable to phone for help.

Dr Goodman asked whether they might call for assistance as he was on his way to see a patient. He wanted to know if there was a motor mechanic in town who might come and help him start the car.

John's mother said that there was no telephone line to their area. It was another two kilometres into the main part of town. By now the mechanic would have closed. It would be difficult to get help for Dr Goodman.

It was getting late and a little dangerous to walk along the edge of the road into town to get help. There were no street lights or footpaths.

Just then, John made a suggestion to his mother. He said that if he rode his bike into town it would be quicker and safer. He could go along the shortcut and the back roads. He had lights on his bike. He would wear the safety vest that the local council had given to all bike riders at his school. He would go directly to the house of Mr Lucas the mechanic and ask him to come over and help. They suggested to Dr Goodman that he should wait at their house. John would fetch the mechanic.

Mrs Ford made the tired doctor a cup of tea. In no time at all, John had returned in the little white van owned by Mr Lucas.

Eventually they managed to get the doctor's car started. Dr Goodman was able to see the patient and get back to the base hospital in the city later that night.

Some weeks later, Dr Goodman passed by their house again. He had stopped by to say thanks to the Ford family for helping him. Dr Goodman came to give a small present to John for his kindness in finding the mechanic that evening. The gift was a parcel of books with a message from Dr Goodman. John enjoyed reading the books.

27. What did John notice on the road?

   ○ He saw the sun setting over the mountains.

   ○ He saw flocks of birds flying home to their nests.

   ○ He saw a speck in the distance.

   ○ He saw the mountains.

28. Why were Mrs Ford and Anna startled?

   ○ They were frightened by the stranger's sudden appearance.

   ○ They were alarmed because the stranger was walking alone.

   ○ They were distressed that something had happened.

   ○ They were worried because it was unusual to see a stranger.

29. 'John made a suggestion' means that he

○ was careful to wear a safety vest when riding a bike.

○ came up with a solution to the problem.

○ knew the shortcut and back roads into town.

○ knew the address of the mechanic.

30. This is a story about

○ the bravery of a young boy.

○ kindness to strangers.

○ solving problems if there is no help.

○ finding help when things go wrong.

END OF TEST

Well done! You have completed the fifth Reading Test.

How did you find these questions? We hope you found them interesting. Revise anything that was hard for you. The next test contains some different questions. Take a long break before doing any more tests.

Use the diagnostic chart on pages 120–121 to see which level of ability you reached. This is only an estimate. Don't be surprised if you answered some difficult questions correctly or even missed some easier questions.

Please note that multiple interpretations are possible for the levels of difficulty of these tasks. Also some questions involve skills from different levels. This is only an initial guide to the approximate level of the reading skill assessed.

Instructions

- As you check the answer for each question, mark it as correct (✓) or incorrect (✗). Mark any questions that you omitted or left out as incorrect (✗) for the moment.
- Then look at how many questions you answered correctly in each level.
- You will be able to see what level you are at by finding the point where you started having consistent difficulty with questions at a certain level. For example, if you answered most questions correctly up to the Intermediate level and then got most questions wrong from then onwards, it is likely your ability is at the Intermediate level. You can ask your parents or your teacher to help you do this if it isn't clear to you.

Am I able to ...

	SKILL	ESTIMATED LEVEL	✓ or ✗
1	Write the location?	Advanced	
2	Find clearly stated information?	Standard	
3	Find a clearly stated detail?	Standard	
4	Infer a desire from the text?	Standard	
5	Find the meaning of a phrase?	Intermediate	
6	Distinguish the title page from the contents and index?	Intermediate	
7	Find the author on a title page?	Intermediate	
8	Identify the contents of a book from the title?	Advanced	
9	Describe a word from a book title?	Intermediate	
10	Make connections between words?	Advanced	
11	Select a title for a passage?	Intermediate	
12	Find the author?	Standard	
13	Identify a rhyming word?	Intermediate	
14	Identify the key location of the story?	Intermediate	
15	Define a word?	Advanced	
16	Note a comparison in the story?	Advanced	
17	Find stated information?	Advanced	
18	Select items mentioned in the passage?	Intermediate	
19	Match an item with an image?	Standard	
20	Infer the character of a person?	Advanced	
21	Identify statements that are true?	Intermediate	
22	Relate a picture to clearly stated information?	Intermediate	
23	Find clearly stated information?	Standard	
24	Define a word?	Advanced	

	SKILL	ESTIMATED LEVEL	✓ or ✗
25	Write the meaning of a short poem?	Advanced	
26	Find clearly stated information?	Intermediate	
27	Relate a detail to the question?	Advanced	
28	Explain a reaction?	Advanced	
29	Describe a person in the story?	Advanced	
30	Report the key theme of a story?	Advanced	
	TOTAL		

This is the last Reading Test. This test has the exact same number of questions as the Year 3 NAPLAN Online Reading Test.
There are 39 questions.

If you aren't sure what to do, ask your teacher or your parents to help you. Don't be afraid to ask if it isn't clear to you.

Allow around 45 minutes for this test.

In this test you will need to look at a picture or read something first. Then read each question and colour in the circle with the correct answer. Sometimes you will instead have to write an answer in the space provided.

Read the description of a person and answer question 1.

Uncle Bluegum has a beard. He wears a green hat and grey shirt.

1. Which picture is of Uncle Bluegum?

Read *The little pine tree* and answer questions 2 to 10.

The little pine tree

A little pine tree was in the woods. It had no leaves. It had needles.

The little tree said, 'I do not like needles. All the other trees in the woods have pretty leaves. I want leaves, too. But I will have better leaves. I want gold leaves.'

Night came and the little tree went to sleep. A fairy came by and gave it gold leaves.

When the little tree woke it had leaves of gold. It said, 'Oh, I am so pretty! No other tree has gold leaves.'

Night came. A man came by with a bag. He saw the gold leaves. He took them all and put them into his bag.

The poor little tree cried, 'I do not want gold leaves again. I will have glass leaves.'

So the little tree went to sleep. The fairy came by and put glass leaves on it. The little tree woke and saw its glass leaves. How pretty they looked in the sunshine! No other tree was so bright.

Then a wind came up. It blew and blew. The glass leaves all fell from the tree and were broken.

Again the little tree had no leaves. It was very sad, and said, 'I will not have gold leaves and I will not have glass leaves. I want green leaves. I want to be like the other trees.'

And the little tree went to sleep. When it woke, it was like other trees. It had green leaves.

A goat came by. He saw the green leaves on the little tree. The goat was hungry and he ate all the leaves.

Then the little tree said, 'I do not want any leaves. I will not have green leaves, nor glass leaves, nor gold leaves. I like my needles best.'

And the little tree went to sleep. The fairy gave it what it wanted. When it woke, it had its needles again. Then the little pine tree was happy.

Source: *A Primary Reader. Old-time Stories, Fairy Tales and Myths Retold by Children* by E Louise Smythe, www.gutenberg.org

2. What are the *needles* in the story?

○ small pins

○ metal leaves

○ very fine leaves

○ small branches

○ pine cones

3. Why did the little pine tree dislike needles?

○ It wanted to be a big tree.

○ It wanted to be a green tree.

○ It wanted to be a tree with leaves.

○ It wanted to be a tree with branches.

4. What leaves did the little pine tree want at first?

○ gold leaves

○ glass leaves

○ green leaves

○ needle leaves

5. Who gave the tree the gold leaves?

the man	the goat	the wind	the fairy
○	○	○	○

6. What happened to the glass leaves?

○ They were burnt by the sun.

○ They were chewed by the goat.

○ They were blown by the wind.

○ They were stolen by the thief.

7. What did the little tree want at the end?

○ gold leaves

○ glass leaves

○ green leaves

○ needles

8. What type of ending does this story have?

   ○ a happy ending

   ○ a funny ending

   ○ a magic ending

   ○ a sad ending

9. Is this a true story?

   likely   unlikely

   ○   ○

10. What is the message of this story?

    ○ You should not make wishes.

    ○ It is always better to be cheerful.

    ○ Sometimes when we make changes, they can lead to bad results.

    ○ You cannot change your life.

Look at the poster and answer questions 11 to 13.

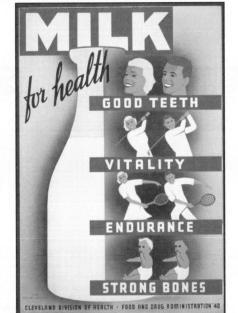

Source: http://upload.wikimedia.org/wikipedia/commons/9/9f/WPAMilkPoster1940.jpg

11. Who is this message mainly for? You can colour in more than one circle.

○ chemists

○ children

○ doctors

○ parents

○ teachers

○ dairy farmers

12. What do you think the poster is saying?

○ It is saying that milk makes you active and helps babies grow and be healthy.

○ It is saying that you need to drink milk to play tennis and golf well.

○ It is saying that if you have problems with your teeth, you can't play tennis.

○ It is telling you to look after your teeth.

13. What is the meaning of the word *vitality* in the poster?

○ skill

○ energy

○ laziness

○ knowledge

It would be a good idea to check your answers to questions 1 to 13 before moving on to the other questions.

Look at the cartoon pictures about a lion and a bug and answer question 14.

14. The pictures are not in the right order. Put the number 1 in the box next to the picture that comes first. Then put the number 2 in the box next to the picture that comes second. Finally put the number 3 in the box next to the picture that comes third.

Source: http://commons.wikimedia.org/wiki/File:Strip_24.jpg

Look carefully at the images below and answer questions 15 to 19.

Source: http://commons.wikimedia.org/wiki/File:Foxygrandpa1904.jpg

15. Why did the boys walk away from the barrel? Colour in one circle.

- ○ They needed help opening the barrel.
- ○ They needed more oranges.
- ○ They were trying to find Grandpa.
- ○ They were afraid of what may have been in there.

16. The boys were surprised because

- ○ they could not open the barrel.
- ○ Grandpa was hiding in the barrel.
- ○ the barrel was heavy.
- ○ the barrel had turned upside down.

17. From these pictures we can tell that

- ○ the boys are not very strong.
- ○ the boys are clever.
- ○ Grandpa likes to play tricks.
- ○ oranges are lighter than a human being.

18. Is this a true story?

- ○ likely
- ○ unlikely

19. Which word would you use to describe the cartoon? You can colour in more than one circle.

- ○ calm
- ○ amusing
- ○ sad
- ○ thankful
- ○ furious
- ○ respectful

Read *What is a comet?* and answer questions 20 to 25.

What is a comet?

It was a warm evening. Michaela went outside with her mother. There was light from the full moon.

She told her mother that they learnt about stars and planets at school today. 'Did you also learn about comets?' her mother asked.

Michaela asked, 'What is a comet?'

'A comet is a bright heavenly body with a tail. They are also part of our solar system,' said her mother. 'Comets are made of dust mixed with chemicals.'

She described how comets move around the sun. We often see a comet when it gets much closer to our planet.

'The path that they travel is called an orbit,' said her mother. 'Their orbits are shaped like an ellipse.'

Michaela's mother drew the shape of an ellipse on a piece of paper for her. An ellipse is like a flattened circle.

'The two main parts of a comet are the head and its tails,' she said. Her mother drew a little figure to show these parts.

'The head of a comet includes the coma and the nucleus. The nucleus is inside the coma. The tails of a comet are very long and bright. They include a dust tail and a gas tail. They are the most well-known part of a comet.'

'How often do comets return?' asked Michaela. Her mother said that the well-known Halley's Comet returns every 76 years. It is next due to appear in 2061.

20 What did Michaela learn about at school today?

○ the sun   ○ the stars   ○ comets

○ meteors   ○ ellipse

> Did you colour in one of the circles?

21. Which of these facts about comets is correct?

○ A comet is a heavenly body.   ○ A comet is a star.

○ A comet is a planet.   ○ A comet is a solar system.

22. What is an *orbit*?

path	planet	direction	speed
○	○	○	○

23. Here is a drawing of a comet. The lines point to the different parts of the comet. Two of the labels have been completed for you. Fill in the two names that are missing.

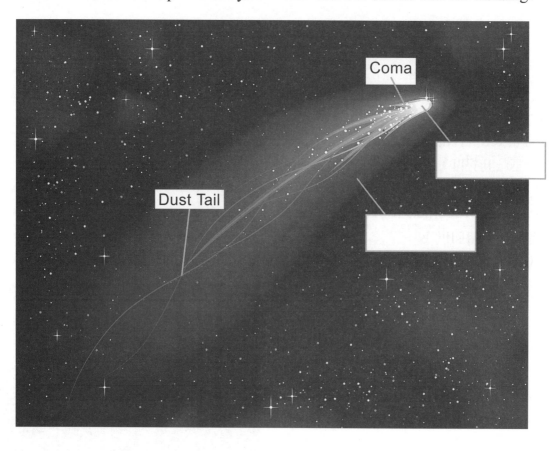

Coma

Dust Tail

24. Read the passage and decide which shape is most like an ellipse.

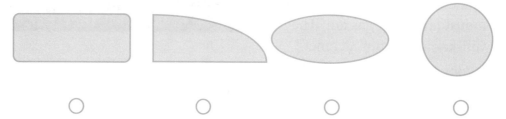

○   ○   ○   ○

25. Does Halley's Comet appear regularly?

yes   no

○   ○

It would be a good idea to check your answers to questions 14 to 25 before moving on to the other questions.

Read *Words from my friend* and answer questions 26 to 30.

Words from my friend

My friend paused, before starting to speak;
Her words were like honey, gentle and meek.
She told of her childhood, the years that went by;
The poverty and hunger brought a tear to her eye.
A miracle saved her, when all seemed so dark;
Planted courage and hope to make a new start.
Her lips trembled slightly, she wept as she spoke;
Flooding my heart, in one single stroke.
I thought that I knew her, how wrong can one be;
The heart of each person is a deep mystery.

26. What type of text is *Words from my friend*?

   story   non-fiction   poem
   ○   ○   ○

27. How did the friend speak?
   ○ She spoke with anger.
   ○ She spoke with happiness.
   ○ She spoke with sadness.

28. What is the meaning of the word *meek* in the second line?

   humble   mighty   soft   silent
   ○   ○   ○   ○

29. What gave the person courage?

   a friend   a miracle   a new start   hope
   ○   ○   ○   ○

30. What is the message of this passage?

○ It is good to have a friend to tell your problems to.

○ Sometimes we do not really know everything about our friends.

○ Hope and courage are needed in life.

Look at the book cover and answer questions 31 and 32.

Source: Wikimedia Commons, http://commons.wikimedia.org/wiki/File:CH01_Abominable_newdesign.jpg

31. What is the name of the author of this book? Colour in one circle.

○ The Abominable Snowman

○ R. A. Montgomery

○ Choose Your Own Adventure

32. How can you choose your own adventure in this book?

○ There are many short stories in the book.

○ You can use your imagination.

○ There are many different endings to the story.

○ It has an interesting and exciting end.

○ There are 24 chapters in the book.

Read *As wise as an owl* and answer questions 33 to 35.

As wise as an owl

Everyone at school trusted Jack. They knew he was honest and fair.

They often came to him for advice. For some reason everyone listened to him and did what he decided. Some children even said that he was as wise as an owl. Others said he was wise like King Solomon.

One day two boys were arguing. Each one was tugging at a cage. They were shouting at each other. They could not agree.

A large group gathered around. Then someone suggested that they take their problem to Jack.

The boys approached Jack's house. The front yard had filled with many children. Word had got around. Adults stopped to look and see what was happening.

The younger boy said, 'Jack, this other boy and I are neighbours. For my birthday I was given a pet bird. It was something that I had wanted for a very long time. Three days later this boy was also given a pet bird.'

'They were exactly the same type of bird. No-one else around here has white cockatoos like these. After a few days this boy's bird died. So, when I was playing cricket, he snuck into my back yard. He put his dead bird in the cage and then took my bird. When I went to feed it the next morning, I realised that it was not the bird I was given.'

The other boy said, 'No! The dead bird is yours. The living one is mine.' They argued in front of Jack.

Jack got up and said in a loud voice to everyone, 'This one says, "My bird is alive, yours is dead." The other says, "No! Yours is dead, and mine is alive."'

Jack went and fetched a sharp knife. He said, 'There is no easy answer. I will now cut the living bird in two and give half to one and half to the other.'

The first boy was filled with great sadness. He said, 'Please Jack, give him the living bird! Please don't kill my bird! It is better if it lives even if I can't keep it!'

But the other boy said, 'Good, neither of us will have the bird. Go ahead and cut it in two!'

Then Jack made his decision. 'Give the living bird to the first boy. We will not kill it because it really is his bird. He loved it so much that he did not want to see it harmed. The other boy didn't really care and was happy to see it killed.'

When everyone in the neighbourhood heard about Jack's decision they were greatly amazed. They saw that he had wisdom and was truly fair.

Adapted from *A wise ruling,* 1 Kings 3: 16–28

33. Who in the story is described as wise? Choose three answers.

○ the first boy

○ King Solomon

○ the adults

○ the parrot

○ the owl

○ Jack

34. Why did Jack suggest that the bird be cut in half?

○ He was honest and fair.

○ to punish the boys for arguing

○ He could not decide who was telling the truth.

○ It was a trick to see who loved the bird.

35. What is the meaning of the word *harmed* in the story?

○ offended

○ injured

○ handled

○ healed

Write your answers to Questions 36 to 39.

---

36. Write the type of bird that is described as wise. _____

37. What colour was the bird that died? _____

38. Give one reason why everyone at school trusted Jack.

_____

39. What was the reaction of everyone in the neighbourhood when they heard of Jack's decision?

_____

END OF TEST

Well done! You have completed the final Reading Test. It means that you have answered or attempted over 135 Reading questions. Now take a long break before you do any more tests.

How did you find the questions in this test? Were some hard for you? Check to see where you did well and where you had problems.

Use the diagnostic chart on pages 136–137 to see which level of ability you reached. This is only an estimate. Don't be surprised if you answered some difficult questions correctly or even missed some easier questions.

Please note that multiple interpretations are possible for the levels of ability of these tasks. Also, some questions involve skills from different levels. This is only an initial guide to the approximate level of the reading skill assessed. No claim is made that this will be identical to the scores a student will receive in the actual tests, as the assessors will use a complex scoring system to estimate a student's level of ability.

Instructions

- As you check the answer for each question, mark it as correct (✓) or incorrect (✗). Mark any questions that you omitted or left out as incorrect (✗) for the moment.

- Then look at how many questions you answered correctly in each level.

- You will be able to see what level you are at by finding the point where you started having consistent difficulty with questions at a certain level. For example, if you answered most questions correctly up to the Intermediate level and then got most questions wrong from then onwards, it is likely your ability is at the Intermediate level. You can ask your parents or your teacher to help you do this if it isn't clear to you.

Am I able to ...

	SKILL	ESTIMATED LEVEL	✓ or ✗
1	Match a picture to a description?	Standard	
2	Define a different use of a common word?	Advanced	
3	Provide a reason?	Intermediate	
4	Find clearly stated information?	Standard	
5	Find clearly stated information?	Standard	
6	Find clearly stated information?	Standard	
7	Find clearly stated information?	Standard	
8	Describe the ending to a story?	Intermediate	
9	Distinguish a fiction story from non-fiction?	Standard	
10	Describe the message of a story?	Advanced	
11	Identify the potential audience for a poster?	Intermediate	
12	State the message in a poster?	Advanced	
13	Define a word?	Advanced	
14	Place cartoons into sequence?	Advanced	
15	Use inference when looking at a cartoon?	Advanced	
16	Find the reason for a situation?	Intermediate	
17	Infer the character of a person?	Advanced	
18	Decide whether a story is true or real?	Standard	
19	Identify the tone of a text?	Advanced	
20	Find an item of clearly stated information?	Standard	
21	Recognise an item of clearly stated information?	Standard	
22	Find clearly stated information?	Standard	
23	Complete a diagram with facts from the text?	Advanced	
24	Find a shape to match a written description?	Advanced	
25	Acknowledge a true statement?	Intermediate	

	SKILL	ESTIMATED LEVEL	✓ or ✗
26	Recognise the form of text?	Standard	
27	Indicate the mood?	Advanced	
28	Define a word?	Advanced	
29	Make a connection to an event?	Advanced	
30	State the meaning of a poem?	Advanced	
31	Find the author of a book?	Standard	
32	Explain the reason for a statement?	Advanced	
33	Identify a quality shared by different characters?	Advanced	
34	Understand the reasons for an action?	Advanced	
35	Find the similar meaning of a word?	Advanced	
36	Locate an item of information in a story?	Intermediate	
37	Locate an item of information in a story?	Intermediate	
38	Provide a reason for an action?	Advanced	
39	Describe a reaction in a story?	Intermediate	
	TOTAL		

This is the first Conventions of Language Test. There are 25 questions.

If you aren't sure what to do, ask your teacher or your parents to help you. Don't be afraid to ask if it isn't clear to you.

Allow around 30 minutes for this test. Take a short break if necessary.

☞ **Tip for Question 1**

An **abbreviation** is a short way of writing something.

Examples

metre = m   Doctor = Dr

1. Write the abbreviation for each word in the box next to it.

Mister ⬜   Street ⬜

Road ⬜   kilometre ⬜

Read the sentences. They are each missing the punctuation mark at the end. Choose the correct punctuation mark to end each sentence. Colour in only one circle for each answer.

2. John played all his favourite games

   ○ .   ○ ?   ○ !

3. Happy Birthday, John

   ○ .   ○ ?   ○ !

4. Why does the word "John" need a capital letter

   ○ .   ○ ?   ○ !

Read the sentences and answer questions 5 to 13.

5. Ella sat up straight in class as the teacher spoke and waited patiently as she handed out the awards.

   Which is a verb (doing word) in this sentence?

   ○ sat ○ up ○ straight ○ patiently ○ awards

6. Which sentence is correct?

   ○ Joe and Jane catches the bus to school each day.

   ○ Joe and Jane catched the bus to school each day.

   ○ Joe and Jane catching the bus to school each day.

   ○ Joe and Jane catch the bus to school each day.

7. Jane ▢▢▢▢▢ forward to seeing all her friends.

   Which word completes the sentence correctly?

   ○ looks ○ looking ○ look

8. Eight of us had to squeeze into the tiny car.

   Which is the pronoun in this sentence?

   ○ us ○ into ○ tiny

9. We played with the rabbit then fed her some carrots.

   Which are the pronouns in this sentence? Colour in more than one circle.

   ○ we ○ rabbit ○ her

10. Which sentence below is correct?

    ○ Sophia rode the horse quite well. ○ Sophia rided the horse quite well.

11. Which sentence below is correct?

    ○ The principal couldn't come to the meeting.

    ○ The principal could'nt come to the meeting.

    ○ The principal couldnt come to the meeting.

12. Which sentence below uses apostrophes where needed?

○ We liked reading Ronald Smith's books.   ○ We liked reading Ronald Smiths' books.

○ We liked reading Ronald Smiths books.

13. Which word completes the sentence correctly?

The [_____] has been horrible this week.

○ whether   ○ weather

To the student

Ask your teacher or parent to read the spelling words for you. The words are listed on page 239. Write the spelling words on the lines below.

Test 1 spelling words

14. _____

15. _____

16. _____

17. _____

18. _____

19. _____

20. _____

21. _____

Read the text _The island_. The spelling mistakes have been underlined.
Write the correct spelling of the word in the box.

The island

Let's explore Kemon Island.
Your help is needed to find the animals.

22. Walk as <u>farst</u> as you can.   [_____]

23. On the <u>beech</u> you will see some seagulls.

24. From the <u>roks</u> you might see dolphins.

25. By the river <u>their</u> are some pelicans.

Did you write your answers in the boxes?

END OF TEST

Well done if you managed to complete the first Conventions of Language Test! We really mean this as there were many questions to answer.

How did you go with these test questions? Some were harder than the practice questions. Check to see where you did well and where you had some problems. Try to revise the questions that were hard for you.

Use the diagnostic chart on page 142 to see which level of ability you reached. This is only an estimate. Don't be surprised if you answered some difficult questions correctly or even missed some easier questions.

Please note that multiple interpretations are possible for the levels of difficulty of these tasks. Also some questions involve skills from different levels. This is only an initial guide to the approximate level of the language skill assessed.

The next Conventions of Language Test contains 30 questions. We will start to include new types of questions in this test.

Instructions

- As you check the answer for each question, mark it as correct (✓) or incorrect (✗). Mark any questions that you omitted or left out as incorrect (✗) for the moment.
- Then look at how many questions you answered correctly in each level.
- You will be able to see what level you are at by finding the point where you started having consistent difficulty with questions at a certain level. For example, if you answered most questions correctly up to the Intermediate level and then got most questions wrong from then onwards, it is likely your ability is at the Intermediate level. You can ask your parents or your teacher to help you do this if it isn't clear to you.

Am I able to ...

	SKILL	ESTIMATED LEVEL	✓ or ✗
1	Write abbreviations for common terms?	Intermediate	
2	Insert a full stop for a statement?	Standard	
3	Insert an exclamation mark for an exclamation?	Advanced	
4	Insert a question mark for a question?	Intermediate	
5	Recognise a verb in a sentence?	Advanced	
6	Match verb and subject?	Advanced	
7	Recognise the correct tense?	Advanced	
8	Identify pronouns?	Advanced	
9	Recognise multiple pronouns in a sentence?	Advanced	
10	Use the correct past tense of a verb?	Standard	
11	Use apostrophes correctly?	Advanced	
12	Use apostrophes to show possession and contraction?	Advanced	
13	Use the correct homophone?	Advanced	
14	Spell *extra*?	Standard	
15	Spell *dress*?	Standard	
16	Spell *collect*?	Standard	
17	Spell *sight*?	Standard	
18	Spell *stood*?	Standard	
19	Spell *fixed*?	Standard	
20	Spell *pay*?	Standard	
21	Spell *goes*?	Standard	
22	Spell *fast*?	Intermediate	
23	Spell *beach*?	Intermediate	
24	Spell *rocks*?	Intermediate	
25	Distinguish *their* from *there*?	Intermediate	
	TOTAL		

This is the second Conventions of Language Test. There are 30 questions.

If you aren't sure what to do, ask your teacher or your parents to help you. Don't be afraid to ask if it isn't clear to you.

Allow around 30 to 40 minutes for this test. Take a short break if necessary.

Read the text *Koala*. It has some gaps. Choose the correct word or words to fill each gap. Colour in only one circle for each answer.

Koala

1. There _____ a time when Koala could not find food.

    is   was   were
    ○   ○   ○

2. There were no leaves _____ anything else to eat.

    and   or   but
    ○   ○   ○

3. Koala said, "I will _____ of hunger.

    die   dead   dying
    ○   ○   ○

4. I _____ go to my uncle."

    will   have   am
    ○   ○   ○

5. He went to where his uncle _____ .

    living   lived   will live
    ○   ○   ○

6. Koala _____ happy with his uncle.

    am   be   was
    ○   ○   ○

7. He decided to ▨▨▨▨ back when he heard there was food.

   go   goes   going
   ○   ○   ○

8. His uncle gave him a present ▨▨▨▨ a slingshot and a flute.

   off   of   for
   ○   ○   ○

Some parts are missing from the sentences below. Colour in the circle with the missing word. Colour in only one circle for each answer.

9. You ▨▨▨▨ hunt for food with the slingshot.

   can   cannot   are
   ○   ○   ○

10. You can ▨▨▨▨ anyone sing with the flute.

   made   makes   make
   ○   ○   ○

Read the sentences and choose the one in each case that is punctuated correctly.

11. ○ My Mother had an Old Mirror.

    ○ My mother had an old Mirror.

    ○ My Mother Had An Old Mirror

    ○ My mother had an old mirror.

12. ○ We Placed It. By The side of the barn.

○ We placed it by the side of the barn.

○ We placed it by. The side of the barn.

○ We placed it by the side of the barn

Read the sentences and answer questions 13 to 15.

13. Which sentence is correct?

○ Scarletts ballet class is an hour long.

○ Scarletts ballet class' is an hour long.

○ Scarlett's ballet class is an hour long.

14. Which sentence is correct?

○ Dimis house has two floors.

○ Dimi's house has two floor's.

○ Dimi's house has two floors.

Did you colour in one of the circles?

15. Which sentence is correct?

○ There was no answer. "How rude!" shouted Maddie.

○ There was no answer "How rude" shouted Maddie.

○ There was no answer. How rude! Shouted Maddie.

To the student

Ask your teacher or parent to read the spelling words for you. The words are listed on page 239. Write the spelling words on the lines below.

✏️ **Test 2 spelling words**

16. _____   21. _____

17. _____   22. _____

18. _____   23. _____

19. _____   24. _____

20. _____   25. _____

Read the text *My new school*. The spelling mistakes have been underlined. Write the correct spelling of the word in the box.

My new school

26. I have been living in the country for <u>wun</u> year.

[   ]

27. I have made <u>sum</u> good friends.

28. I play the <u>trumpat</u>.

29. Many people come to <u>heer</u> my band.

30. I play songs they like <u>agen</u>.

Did you write the correct word in the box?

END OF TEST

Well done if you managed to complete the second Conventions of Language Test! We really mean this as there were many questions to answer.

How did you go with these test questions? Some were harder than the practice questions. Check to see where you did well and where you had some problems. Try to revise the questions that were hard for you.

Use the diagnostic chart on page 148 to see which level of ability you reached. This is only an estimate. Don't be surprised if you answered some difficult questions correctly or even missed some easier questions.

Please note that multiple interpretations are possible for the levels of difficulty of these tasks. Also some questions involve skills from different levels. This is only an initial guide to the approximate level of the language skill assessed.

The next Conventions of Language Test contains 35 questions. We will include new types of questions in this test.

Instructions

- As you check the answer for each question, mark it as correct (✓) or incorrect (✗). Mark any questions that you omitted or left out as incorrect (✗) for the moment.

- Then look at how many questions you answered correctly in each level.

- You will be able to see what level you are at by finding the point where you started having consistent difficulty with questions at a certain level. For example, if you answered most questions correctly up to the Intermediate level and then got most questions wrong from then onwards, it is likely your ability is at the Intermediate level. You can ask your parents or your teacher to help you do this if it isn't clear to you.

Am I able to ...

	SKILL	ESTIMATED LEVEL	✓ or ✗
1	Use the past tense?	Intermediate	
2	Use a conjunction?	Intermediate	
3	Use the correct tense?	Intermediate	
4	Use the future tense?	Intermediate	
5	Match verb and subject?	Intermediate	
6	Use the correct tense?	Advanced	
7	Use the infinitive?	Advanced	
8	Use the correct preposition?	Advanced	
9	Recognise the correct tense?	Intermediate	
10	Recognise the correct tense?	Intermediate	
11	Recognise correct punctuation?	Intermediate	
12	Recognise correct punctuation?	Intermediate	
13	Use apostrophes correctly?	Intermediate	
14	Use apostrophes to show possession?	Intermediate	
15	Use correct speech punctuation?	Advanced	
16	Spell *army*?	Intermediate	
17	Spell *pretty*?	Intermediate	
18	Spell *would*?	Intermediate	
19	Spell *could*?	Intermediate	
20	Spell *week*?	Standard	
21	Spell *twice*?	Intermediate	
22	Spell *first*?	Intermediate	
23	Spell *hour*?	Intermediate	
24	Spell *seem*?	Standard	
25	Spell *might*?	Intermediate	
26	Spell *one*?	Standard	
27	Spell *some*?	Standard	
28	Spell *trumpet*?	Standard	
29	Spell *hear*?	Standard	
30	Spell *again*?	Standard	
	TOTAL		

ADAPTED FOR
ONLINE
FORMAT

This is the third Conventions of Language Test. There are 35 questions.

If you aren't sure what to do, ask your teacher or your parents to help you. Don't be afraid to ask if it isn't clear to you.

Allow around 35 to 45 minutes for this test. Take a short break if necessary.

Read the text *The bay*. It has some gaps. Choose the correct word or words to fill each gap. Colour in only one circle for each answer.

The bay

1. Ying and his family _____ to go for a walk.

            like   likes
             ○   ○

2. The sun is setting _____ the horizon.

          in   on   by
        ○   ○   ○

3. Everything _____ peaceful.

          are   is   am
        ○   ○   ○

4. They walk to the beach, _____ around the shore.

when	but	then
○	○	○

5. The water is _____ and it covers the rocks.

high	higher	highest
○	○	○

6. Many people _____ fishing.

is	are	am
○	○	○

7. Some fishermen stand in the water and are up to _____ waist.

there	their
○	○

8. Others are looking _____ prawns.

for	at	to
○	○	○

9. They shine a light in the water _____ carry a net.

and	but
○	○

10. Pelicans wait ▓▓▓▓▓ the rocks.

to	by	for
○	○	○

11. A boy ▓▓▓▓▓ his small boat in a rock pool.

sai	sails	sailing
○	○	○

Read the sentences and answer questions 12 to 19.

12. ▓▓▓▓▓ been raining for many ▓▓▓▓▓ in Queensland.

Which words complete the sentence correctly?

○ Its week's

○ It's week's

○ It's weeks

13. Our ▓▓▓▓▓ main street was a river of mud.

Which word completes the sentence correctly?

○ town

○ towns

○ town's

14. Which sentence is correct?

○ Police had to rescue families?

○ Police had to rescue families;

○ Police had to rescue families,

○ Police had to rescue families.

Did you colour in one of the circles?

15. Many people in Queensland are still missing.

The word *Many* is

○ a noun.　　○ an adjective.　　○ an adverb.　　○ a verb.

16. Which of these is a complete statement?

○ Going to Queensland

○ I will be coming.

○ Hope how will.

17. Mrs Sios loved her new office ▭ she didn't like the view.

Choose the correct word to fill the gap in this sentence.

○ but

○ and

○ so

18. We drove to the seaside ▭ it took an hour to get there.

Choose the correct word to fill the gap in this sentence.

○ but

○ and

○ so

19. ▭ new classrooms are built then we will lose part of our playground.

Choose the correct word to fill the gap in this sentence.

○ If

○ As

○ Of

○ How

Did you colour in one of the circles?

To the student

Ask your teacher or parent to read the spelling words for you. The words are listed on page 239. Write the spelling words on the lines below.

Test 3 spelling words

20. _____   25. _____

21. _____   26. _____

22. _____   27. _____

23. _____   28. _____

24. _____   29. _____

Read the sentences. The spelling mistakes have been underlined. Write the correct spelling of the word in the box.

30. I will draw a <u>skware</u>.

31. I will not <u>choos</u> a circle.

32. <u>Toonight</u> is Halloween.

33. My mother will <u>alow</u> me to go.

34. I will <u>friten</u> people.

35. I have a mask and a <u>blac</u> cloak.

Did you write the correct word in the box?

END OF TEST

Well done if you managed to complete the third Conventions of Language Test! We really mean this as there were many questions to answer.

How did you go with these test questions? Some were harder than the practice questions. Check to see where you did well and where you had some problems. Try to revise the questions that were hard for you.

Use the diagnostic chart on pages 155–156 to see which level of ability you reached. This is only an estimate. Don't be surprised if you answered some difficult questions correctly or even missed some easier questions.

Please note that multiple interpretations are possible for the levels of difficulty of these tasks. Also some questions involve skills from different levels. This is only an initial guide to the approximate level of the language skill assessed.

The next Conventions of Language Test contains 40 questions. We will include new types of questions in this test.

Instructions

- As you check the answer for each question, mark it as correct (✓) or incorrect (✖). Mark any questions that you omitted or left out as incorrect (✖) for the moment.
- Then look at how many questions you answered correctly in each level.
- You will be able to see what level you are at by finding the point where you started having consistent difficulty with questions at a certain level. For example, if you answered most questions correctly up to the Intermediate level and then got most questions wrong from then onwards, it is likely your ability is at the Intermediate level. You can ask your parents or your teacher to help you do this if it isn't clear to you.

Am I able to ...

	SKILL	ESTIMATED LEVEL	✓ or ✖
1	Match verb and subject?	Intermediate	
2	Use a preposition?	Intermediate	
3	Match verb and subject?	Intermediate	
4	Use the correct preposition?	Advanced	
5	Recognise the correct word?	Intermediate	
6	Recognise the correct verb for a collective noun?	Intermediate	
7	Use a personal pronoun?	Intermediate	
8	Use a preposition correctly?	Intermediate	
9	Use the correct preposition?	Intermediate	
10	Use a preposition correctly?	Intermediate	
11	Match subject and verb?	Intermediate	
12	Use the apostrophe correctly to show contraction?	Intermediate	
13	Use apostrophes to show possession?	Intermediate	
14	Recognise sentence punctuation?	Intermediate	
15	Identify an adjective?	Intermediate	
16	Recognise a complete sentence?	Intermediate	
17	Use the correct conjunction in a sentence?	Intermediate	
18	Identify the correct conjunction to form a compound sentence?	Intermediate	
19	Use a conjunction to introduce a clause?	Intermediate	
20	Spell *story*?	Intermediate	
21	Spell *without*?	Intermediate	
22	Spell *wife*?	Standard	
23	Spell *head*?	Intermediate	
24	Spell *open*?	Standard	
25	Spell *short*?	Standard	

	SKILL	ESTIMATED LEVEL	✓ or ✗
26	Spell *round*?	Standard	
27	Spell *become*?	Standard	
28	Spell *reach*?	Intermediate	
29	Spell *price*?	Intermediate	
30	Spell *square*?	Standard	
31	Spell *choose*?	Intermediate	
32	Spell *tonight*?	Standard	
33	Spell *allow*?	Intermediate	
34	Spell *frighten*?	Advanced	
35	Spell *black*?	Standard	
	TOTAL		

An important note about the NAPLAN Online tests

The NAPLAN Online Conventions of Language test will be divided into different sections. Students will only have one opportunity to check their answers at the end of each section before proceeding to the next one. This means that after students have completed a section and moved onto the next they will not be able to check their work again. We have included reminders for students to check their work at specific points in the practice tests from now on so they become familiar with this process.

This is the fourth Conventions of Language Test. There are 40 questions.

If you aren't sure what to do, ask your teacher or your parents to help you. Don't be afraid to ask if it isn't clear to you.

Allow around 40 to 45 minutes for this test. Take a short break if necessary.

Read the text *A new school*. It has some gaps. Choose the correct word or words to fill each gap. Colour in only one circle for each answer.

A new school

1. Anthony _____ John are the brothers of Nicholas.

   or ○   and ○   with ○

2. Nicholas and his brothers _____ to different high schools.

   went ○   goes ○   am going ○

3. Nicholas used to live at _____ .

   ○ 85 ocean Street   ○ 85 Ocean street   ○ 85 Ocean Street

4. Nicholas's new school is _____ .

   ○ St Mary's High School   ○ St Marys' high school   ○ st mary's high school

5. It is now _____ for Nicholas to go to school by bus.

   quicker ○   quickly ○   more quicker ○

6. The teacher said, _____
   - ○ you will need a bus pass.
   - ○ "You will need a bus pass."
   - ○ "you will need a bus pass."

7. _____ mother drives him to school when he has three bags to carry.

   He ○   Him ○   His ○

Colour in the circle with the correct answer.

8. Which sentence is correct?

   ○ Mary-Ellen who is aged eight is my new schoolfriend.

   ○ Mary-Ellen, who is aged eight, is my new schoolfriend.

   ○ Mary-Ellen who is aged eight, is my new, schoolfriend.

Read the following sentence and answer questions 9 to 11.

The striped cat hurried along the winding path to get to the back of the fish shop.

9. The word *hurried* is

   ○ a noun.　　　　○ an adjective.　　　　○ an adverb.　　　　○ a verb.

10. The word *striped* is

   ○ a noun.　　　　○ an adjective.　　　　○ an adverb.　　　　○ a verb.

11. The word *shop* is

   ○ a noun.　　　　○ an adjective.　　　　○ an adverb.　　　　○ a verb.

Read the following sentences and answer questions 12 to 18.

12 I threw the ball and Wally ran after it.

   Which of these is a pronoun in this sentence? Colour in two answers.

   ○ I　　　　　　○ ball　　　　　　○ Wally　　　　　　○ it

13 `It is raining [_____] can't go to the beach.

   Choose the correct word to fill the gap in this sentence.

   ○ if　　　　　　○ but　　　　　　○ because　　　　　　○ so

14. Pia said, "My eyesight is better than yours!"

The word *than* is used to

○ join.   ○ question.   ○ disagree.   ○ compare.

15. Which sentence is correct?

○ Lydia lost her tooth in class.

○ Lydia lose her tooth in class.

○ Lydia losed her tooth in class.

Did you colour in one of the circles?

16. Which sentence is correct?

○ Its important that youre ready before going to Mias house to swim.

○ It's important that youre ready before going to Mia's house to swim.

○ It's important that you're ready before going to Mia's house to swim.

17. Which of these is a complete statement?

○ coming to visit

○ Nick is coming.

○ to visit this weekend

18. We have an umbrella ▨▨▨▨ it is raining.

Choose the correct word to fill the gap in this sentence.

○ but

○ because

○ so

It would be a good idea to check your answers to questions 1 to 18 before moving on to the other questions.

To the student

Ask your teacher or parent to read the spelling words for you. The words are listed on page 240. Write the spelling words on the lines below.

✏️ **Test 4 spelling words**

19. _____   25. _____

20. _____   26. _____

21. _____   27. _____

22. _____   28. _____

23. _____   29. _____

24. _____   30. _____

Read the text *The concert*. The spelling mistakes have been underlined. Write the correct spelling for each word in the box.

The concert

31. Mrs Smith gave me a long poem to <u>lern</u>.   ☐

32. I practised each <u>verss</u>.   ☐

33. I did this <u>togetha</u> with my mother.

34. There was a <u>larj</u> crowd at the concert.

35. I went <u>strait</u> to the front of the stage.

36. It felt <u>relly</u> good once I finished.

37. The audience <u>clapd</u>.

38. At the end my <u>throte</u> was dry.

39. I felt a little <u>therstee</u>.

40. I said "Thank you" to my <u>teacha</u>.

Did you write the correct word in the box?

END OF TEST

We increased the number of questions in this test. How did you cope with the extra questions? Well done if you managed to complete them all! We really mean this as there were harder questions to answer.

Check to see where you did well and where you had some problems. Try to revise the questions that were hard for you.

Use the diagnostic chart on pages 162–163 to see which level of ability you reached. This is only an estimate. Don't be surprised if you answered some difficult questions correctly or even missed some easier questions.

Please note that multiple interpretations are possible for the levels of difficulty of these tasks. Also some questions involve skills from different levels. This is only an initial guide to the approximate level of the language skill assessed.

The next Conventions of Language Test contains 45 questions. We will include new types of questions in this test.

Instructions

- As you check the answer for each question, mark it as correct (✓) or incorrect (✗). Mark any questions that you omitted or left out as incorrect (✗) for the moment.

- Then look at how many questions you answered correctly in each level.

- You will be able to see what level you are at by finding the point where you started having consistent difficulty with questions at a certain level. For example, if you answered most questions correctly up to the Intermediate level and then got most questions wrong from then onwards, it is likely your ability is at the Intermediate level. You can ask your parents or your teacher to help you do this if it isn't clear to you..

Am I able to ...

	SKILL	ESTIMATED LEVEL	✓ or ✗
1	Use a conjunction correctly?	Intermediate	
2	Use the past tense and the third person?	Intermediate	
3	Place capital letters in an address?	Standard	
4	Place capital letters in a title?	Intermediate	
5	Use a comparative adjective correctly?	Intermediate	
6	Insert speech marks?	Intermediate	
7	Use the correct personal pronoun?	Intermediate	
8	Insert commas before and after a clause?	Intermediate	
9	Identify a verb?	Intermediate	
10	Recognise an adjective?	Intermediate	
11	Determine which word in a sentence is a noun?	Advanced	
12	Recognise a pronoun?	Advanced	
13	Use the correct conjunction?	Intermediate	
14	Identify the purpose of a conjunction?	Advanced	
15	Recognise the correct past-tense form of a verb?	Intermediate	
16	Use apostrophes to show contraction and possession?	Advanced	
17	Recognise a statement?	Advanced	
18	Identify the correct conjunction for a sentence?	Advanced	
19	Spell *cost*?	Intermediate	
20	Spell *class*?	Intermediate	
21	Spell *care*?	Advanced	
22	Spell *move*?	Intermediate	
23	Spell *behind*?	Advanced	
24	Spell *burn*?	Advanced	
25	Spell *clean*?	Intermediate	

	SKILL	ESTIMATED LEVEL	✓ or ✗
26	Spell *spell*?	Standard	
27	Spell *poor*?	Intermediate	
28	Spell *finish*?	Standard	
29	Spell *hurt*?	Intermediate	
30	Spell *around*?	Standard	
31	Spell *learn*?	Standard	
32	Spell *verse*?	Intermediate	
33	Spell *together*?	Standard	
34	Spell *large*?	Intermediate	
35	Spell *straight*?	Standard	
36	Spell *really*?	Intermediate	
37	Spell *clapped*?	Intermediate	
38	Spell *throat*?	Intermediate	
39	Spell *thirsty*?	Intermediate	
40	Spell *teacher*?	Intermediate	
	TOTAL		

This is the fifth Conventions of Language Test. There are 45 questions.

If you aren't sure what to do, ask your teacher or your parents to help you. Don't be afraid to ask if it isn't clear to you.

Allow around 45 minutes for this test. Take a short break if necessary.

Colour in one circle to show your answer.

1. Which sentence is plural (more than one person)?

   ○ I like the beach in Coogee.

   ○ He likes the beach in Coogee.

   ○ They like the beach in Coogee.

2. Yesterday the sea was very smooth.
   The word *smooth* is

   ○ a noun.   ○ an adjective.   ○ an adverb.   ○ a verb.

Choose the correct word to fill the gap in each sentence.

3. I like to ▢▢▢ by the edge of the water.

   ○ sit

   ○ sat

   ○ sitting

4. I ▢▢▢ some fish with long black tails.

   ○ caught

   ○ catching

   ○ catched

Did you colour in one
of the circles?

5. The fish then ▢▢▢ out of the water.

   ○ leap

   ○ leaping

   ○ leapt

Read the following sentences and answer questions 6 to 10.

6. The big yellow buses were going into town.

   Write this sentence in the singular form in the space provided.

7. Which sentence below is correctly punctuated?

   ○ "The driver said, Hurry along!"

   ○ The driver said, Hurry along!

   ○ The driver said, "Hurry along"

   ○ The driver said, "Hurry along!"

8. Which sentence below is correctly punctuated?

   ○ George Alex and Peter got on the bus.

   ○ George, Alex and Peter got on the bus.

   ○ George, Alex, and Peter, got on the bus.

9. We travel to the beach on this bus.

   Write this sentence in the past tense in the space provided. Past tense means 'as though it happened yesterday'.

10. After we get off the bus we will have some lunch.

    Write this sentence in the past tense in the space provided.

Colour in one circle to show your answer.

11. Nicholas is stronger at chess than Michaela is.

The word *than* is used to

○ join.

○ question.

○ disagree.

○ compare.

12. Which of these is a complete statement?

○ My favourite car is a convertible.

○ Is my favourite car a convertible?

13. Emilio finds it as quick to ride his bike as to walk to work.

The word *as* is used to

○ join.

○ question.

○ disagree.

○ compare.

Now try these. Write your answer in the space provided.

14. Sleep is to sleeping as sit is to

15. Smile is to smiled as walk is to

16. Ear is to ears as eye is to

17. Run is to ran as ring is to

18. I is to we as he is to

19. Which sentence is correct?

○ I tidied Johns' bedroom.

○ I tidied Johns bedroom.

○ I tidied John's bedroom.

20. The windows ⬚⬚⬚ to be cleaned.

Choose the correct word to fill the gap in this sentence.

○ needs

○ need

21. Which sentence is correct?

○ My mother and me swept the floor.

○ My mother and I swept the floor.

○ My mother and we swept the floor.

Did you colour in one of the circles?

It would be a good idea to check your answers to questions 1 to 21 before moving on to the other questions.

To the student

Ask your teacher or parent to read the spelling words for you. The words are listed on page 240. Write the spelling words on the lines below.

✏️ Test 5 spelling words

22. _____

23. _____

24. _____

25. _____

26. _____

27. _____

28. _____

29. _____

30. _____

31. _____

32. _____

33. _____

Read the text *Sounds at night*. The spelling mistake in each sentence is underlined. Write the correct spelling of the underlined word in each box.

Sounds at night

34. It was late at <u>nihgt</u> when I woke from my sleep.

35. There were <u>noyses</u> in the street.

36. This was a <u>serprise</u>.

[ ]

Did you write the correct word in the box?

37. The sounds came from a house <u>ferther</u> down.

[ ]

38. I heard the <u>siron</u> of an ambulance.

[ ]

39. A <u>crowed</u> had gathered.

[ ]

There is one spelling mistake in each sentence. Write the correct spelling of the word in each box.

40. Alltogether seven people came to help.

[ ]

41. A cairless driver had crashed into a house.

[ ]

42. Ambulance workas helped the owner of the house.

[ ]

43. He was very unwel.

44. The ambulance officers spoke to him kinedly.

45. He smiled and thanked them for their help.

END OF TEST

We increased the number of questions again. Are you finding it easier to cope with the extra questions? Once again there were some harder questions to answer. Well done if you managed to complete them all!

Check to see where you did well and where you had problems. Try to revise the questions that were hard for you.

Use the diagnostic chart on pages 171–172 to see which level of ability you reached. This is only an estimate. Don't be surprised if you answered some difficult questions correctly or even missed some easier questions.

Please note that multiple interpretations are possible for the levels of difficulty of these tasks. Also some questions involve skills from different levels. This is only an initial guide to the approximate level of the language skill assessed.

The final Conventions of Language Test contains 50 questions. We will include new types of questions in this test.

Instructions

- As you check the answer for each question, mark it as correct (✓) or incorrect (✗). Mark any questions that you omitted or left out as incorrect (✗) for the moment.
- Then look at how many questions you answered correctly in each level.
- You will be able to see what level you are at by finding the point where you started having consistent difficulty with questions at a certain level. For example, if you answered most questions correctly up to the Intermediate level and then got most questions wrong from then onwards, it is likely your ability is at the Intermediate level. You can ask your parents or your teacher to help you do this if it isn't clear to you.

Am I able to ...

	SKILL	ESTIMATED LEVEL	✓ or ✗
1	Recognise a sentence in the plural form?	Intermediate	
2	Recognise part of a sentence?	Standard	
3	Use the correct verb form?	Advanced	
4	Use the correct tense?	Advanced	
5	Use verbs in the past tense?	Advanced	
6	Place a sentence in the singular form?	Intermediate	
7	Use speech marks correctly?	Intermediate	
8	Use commas to separate items?	Advanced	
9	Place a sentence in the past tense?	Intermediate	
10	Change a sentence from the present to the past tense?	Intermediate	
11	Recognise the use of the comparative?	Intermediate	
12	Identify a complete statement?	Intermediate	
13	Recognise the function of the comparative?	Intermediate	
14	Use the present participle?	Advanced	
15	Convert to the past tense?	Intermediate	
16	Insert a plural noun in an analogy?	Advanced	
17	Use the past tense in an analogy?	Intermediate	
18	Use the third person plural?	Intermediate	
19	Recognise the correct use of an apostrophe for possession?	Intermediate	
20	Match subject and verb?	Advanced	
21	Use the first-person pronoun as a subject?	Intermediate	
22	Spell *clear*?	Intermediate	
23	Spell *maybe*?	Intermediate	
24	Spell *across*?	Standard	
25	Spell *tonight*?	Standard	

	SKILL	ESTIMATED LEVEL	✓ or ✗
26	Spell *tenth*?	Intermediate	
27	Spell *see*?	Intermediate	
28	Spell *these*?	Intermediate	
29	Spell *those*?	Advanced	
30	Spell *full*?	Advanced	
31	Spell *eight*?	Standard	
32	Spell *please*?	Intermediate	
33	Spell *money*?	Intermediate	
34	Spell *night*?	Standard	
35	Spell *noises*?	Standard	
36	Spell *surprise*?	Advanced	
37	Spell *further*?	Advanced	
38	Spell *siren*?	Standard	
39	Spell *crowd*?	Standard	
40	Spell *Altogether*?	Advanced	
41	Spell *careless*?	Intermediate	
42	Spell *workers*?	Intermediate	
43	Spell *unwell*?	Intermediate	
44	Spell *kindly*?	Intermediate	
45	Spell *smiled*?	Intermediate	
	TOTAL		

This is the last Conventions of Language Test. This test has the exact same number of questions as the Year 3 NAPLAN Online Conventions of Language Test. There are 50 questions.

If you aren't sure what to do, ask your teacher or your parents to help you. Don't be afraid to ask if it isn't clear to you.

Allow around 45 minutes for this test. Take a short break if necessary.

Read the text Fred the fixer. In questions 1 to 4 there is an error in each sentence. Write the correct word or words in each box.

Fred the fixer

1. Mr tiding is our friend.

2. He fix cars.

3. There are five cars in Freds garage.

4. we always go to his workshop.

There is a mistake in each sentence in questions 5 to 7. Colour in the circle next to the correct word.

5. He knews everything about cars.

knows ○   knowed ○   knowing ○

6. He taked his time to do a good job.

taked ○   takes ○

7. You can rely upon he.

him ○   his ○

Read the sentences. Colour in the circle or circles where there is a mistake. Be careful: some sentences have more than one mistake.

8. Three capital letters have been left out of this sentence. Which words should start with a capital letter?

the australian team played italy in the final.

9. Two full stops (.) have been left out of these sentences. Where do the missing full stops go?

He comes home He will rest

10. One full stop (.) has been left out of these sentences. Where does the missing full stop go?

I am happy to learn something new It is always interesting.
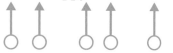

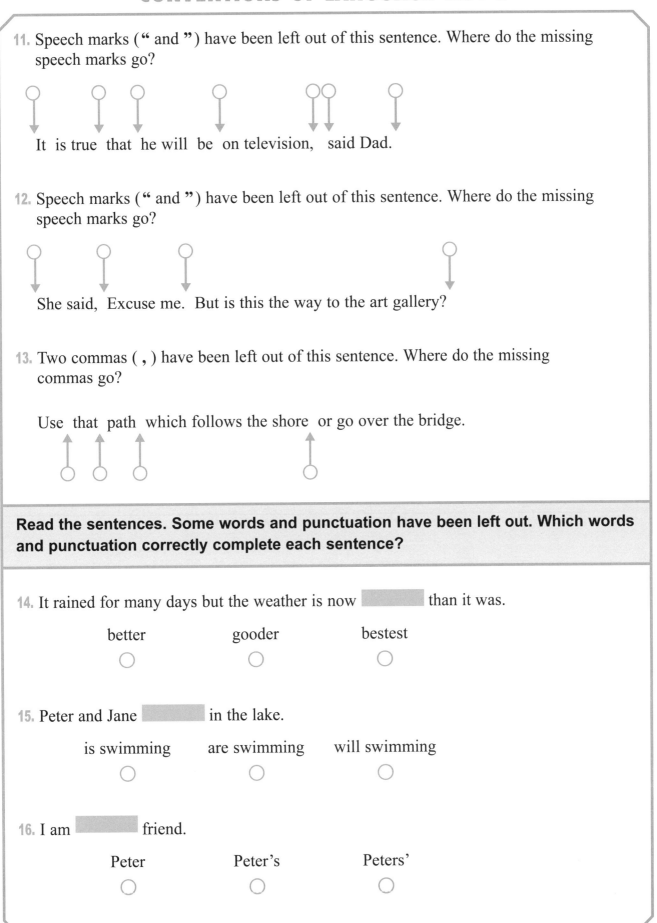

11. Speech marks (" and ") have been left out of this sentence. Where do the missing speech marks go?

It is true that he will be on television, said Dad.

12. Speech marks (" and ") have been left out of this sentence. Where do the missing speech marks go?

She said, Excuse me. But is this the way to the art gallery?

13. Two commas (,) have been left out of this sentence. Where do the missing commas go?

Use that path which follows the shore or go over the bridge.

Read the sentences. Some words and punctuation have been left out. Which words and punctuation correctly complete each sentence?

14. It rained for many days but the weather is now _____ than it was.

better	gooder	bestest
○	○	○

15. Peter and Jane _____ in the lake.

is swimming	are swimming	will swimming
○	○	○

16. I am _____ friend.

Peter	Peter's	Peters'
○	○	○

17. Jane, who is in third class ▮▮▮▮▮ used to go to our school.

,	.	?	!
○	○	○	○

18. Peter is the ▮▮▮▮▮ in the family.

youngest	most young	more younger
○	○	○

19. Peter and ▮▮▮▮▮ went to the same infants school.

me	I	we
○	○	○

20. Both ▮▮▮▮▮ were in the same class.

of us	of we	of our
○	○	○

21. ▮▮▮▮▮ walked to school.

He and I	Him and me	Him and I
○	○	○

22. We would pass under a very big sign that said, ▮▮▮▮▮

○ "Maroubra Junction School"

○ Maroubra Junction School.

○ "Maroubra Junction School".

Did you colour in one of the circles?

23. It is a big sign so that it is ▨▨▨ for drivers to see.

      more easy   easy   more easiest
        ○   ○   ○

24. The school has red and green as ▨▨▨ colours.

      its'   its   it's
        ○   ○   ○

25. The four houses in our school ▨▨▨ Patterson, Lawson, Gordon and Kendall.

      are   am   is
        ○   ○   ○

It would be a good idea to check your answers to questions 1 to 25 before moving on to the other questions.

To the student

Ask your teacher or parent to read the spelling words for you. The words are listed on page 240. Write the spelling words on the lines below.

Test 6 spelling words

26. _____		**34.** _____	
27. _____		**35.** _____	
28. _____		**36.** _____	
29. _____		**37.** _____	
30. _____		**38.** _____	
31. _____		**39.** _____	
32. _____		**40.** _____	
33. _____			

Read the text *A school trip* and answer questions 41 to 45. The spelling mistake in each sentence is underlined. Write the correct spelling of the underlined word in the box.

A school trip

41. We <u>caim</u> to school early.

42. There were six <u>studants</u> in our group.

43. We went on a school <u>excurshon</u>.

Did you write the correct word in the box?

44. We had <u>tuff</u> boots for walking.

45. Our backpacks were very <u>hevy</u>.

For questions 46 to 50 there is a spelling mistake in each sentence. Write the correct spelling of the incorrect word in the box.

46. We camped under some larj trees.

47. We gatherd wood for a small fire.

48. Our meal was mainly cand foods.

49. It was quite dellishus.

50. It was a new adventuer.

END OF TEST

Well done if you completed this last test! It means that you have answered or attempted more than 200 Conventions of Language questions.

We increased the number of questions again this time. Did you find it easy to cope with the extra questions? Once again there were some harder questions to answer.

Use the diagnostic chart on pages 180–181 to see which level of ability you reached. This is only an estimate. Don't be surprised if you answered some difficult questions correctly or even missed some easier questions.

Please note that multiple interpretations are possible for the levels of difficulty of these tasks. Also some questions involve skills from different levels. This is only an initial guide to the approximate level of the language skill assessed.

This was the last Conventions of Language Test. Now take a long break.

Instructions

- As you check the answer for each question, mark it as correct (✓) or incorrect (✗). Mark any questions that you omitted or left out as incorrect (✗) for the moment.
- Then look at how many questions you answered correctly in each level.
- You will be able to see what level you are at by finding the point where you started having consistent difficulty with questions at a certain level. For example, if you answered most questions correctly up to the Intermediate level and then got most questions wrong from then onwards, it is likely your ability is at the Intermediate level. You can ask your parents or your teacher to help you do this if it isn't clear to you.

Am I able to ...

	SKILL	ESTIMATED LEVEL	✓ or ✗
1	Use capital letters for a name?	Standard	
2	Match subject and verb?	Intermediate	
3	Use an apostrophe for possession?	Intermediate	
4	Insert a capital letter at the beginning of a sentence?	Intermediate	
5	Match subject and verb?	Intermediate	
6	Match subject and verb?	Intermediate	
7	Insert a pronoun?	Intermediate	
8	Insert a capital letter for proper nouns?	Intermediate	
9	Insert full stops at the end of sentences?	Standard	
10	Insert full stops at the end of sentences?	Standard	
11	Insert speech marks?	Intermediate	
12	Insert speech marks?	Advanced	
13	Insert commas before and after a clause?	Advanced	
14	Use a comparative adjective?	Intermediate	
15	Match a verb with a compound subject?	Advanced	
16	Use an apostrophe for possession?	Intermediate	
17	Insert a comma after a clause?	Advanced	
18	Use a superlative adjective?	Advanced	
19	Insert a pronoun to match a verb?	Advanced	
20	Insert a preposition and pronoun?	Advanced	
21	Use a combination of pronouns?	Advanced	
22	Use speech marks and a full stop?	Advanced	
23	Use an adjective?	Advanced	
24	Select an appropriate pronoun?	Intermediate	
25	Match subject and verb?	Intermediate	

	SKILL	ESTIMATED LEVEL	✓ or ✗
26	Spell *live*?	Standard	
27	Spell *light*?	Standard	
28	Spell *cloud*?	Advanced	
29	Spell *space*?	Advanced	
30	Spell *queen*?	Intermediate	
31	Spell *sew*?	Intermediate	
32	Spell *coming*?	Intermediate	
33	Spell *sign*?	Intermediate	
34	Spell *easy*?	Advanced	
35	Spell *hopping*?	Advanced	
36	Spell *hotel*?	Intermediate	
37	Spell *draw*?	Intermediate	
38	Spell *window*?	Advanced	
39	Spell *mouth*?	Advanced	
40	Spell *goose*?	Intermediate	
41	Spell *came*?	Intermediate	
42	Spell *students*?	Intermediate	
43	Spell *excursion*?	Advanced	
44	Spell *tough*?	Advanced	
45	Spell *heavy*?	Intermediate	
46	Spell *large*?	Standard	
47	Spell *gathered*?	Intermediate	
48	Spell *canned*?	Intermediate	
49	Spell *delicious*?	Intermediate	
50	Spell *adventure*?	Standard	
	TOTAL		

Check the Writing section (www.nap.edu.au/naplan/writing) of the official NAPLAN website for up-to-date and important information on the Writing Test. Sample Writing Tests and marking guidelines that outline the criteria markers use when assessing your writing are also provided. Please note that, to date in NAPLAN, the types of texts that students have been tested on have been narrative and persuasive writing.

The Australian Curriculum for English requires students to be taught three main types of texts:

- imaginative writing (including narratives and descriptions)
- informative writing (including procedures and reports)
- persuasive writing (expositions).

Informative writing has not yet been tested by NAPLAN. The best preparation for writing is for students to read a range of texts and to get lots of practice in writing different types of texts. We have included information on all types of texts in this book.

About the test

The NAPLAN Writing Test examines a student's ability to write effectively in a specific type of text. Students will come across a number of types of texts at school.

There is only one Writing question in the NAPLAN Writing Test. Students will be provided with some stimulus material that acts as a prompt to writing: something to read or a picture to look at. The student's response will be written on supplied paper.

The NAPLAN Online Writing Test

For the Year 3 NAPLAN Writing Test, unlike the other year levels, students will not use a digital device (a computer or tablet); they will write their answer on paper.

Marking the Writing Test

When the markers of the NAPLAN Writing Test assess students' writing they will mark it according to various criteria. Knowing what they look for will help you understand what to look out for in your own child's writing.

The emphasis is on the quality of expression and what the student has to say. Some features that may be emphasised are:

- the quality of the content
- what the student thinks about the topic
- what feelings are developed
- how it is structured
- whether the writing is organised clearly, using paragraphs and appropriate sequencing
- whether the writing is cohesive
- the quality of the spelling, punctuation and grammar.

Advice for parents and teachers

The aim of this section of the book is to introduce students to a selection of writing tests and to help them begin to write effectively. It is not important at this stage that they write a great deal. This will come with time and practice.

These writing questions will simply help students get used to writing questions and learn how to deal with them. Our *Excel Year 3 NAPLAN* Online–style Tests* book will focus more on in-depth preparation for the test.

In the writing questions found here, students will be given some information that they will need to look at or read. It could be a photograph, a diagram, a drawing or another image. This will help give them ideas for their writing. They will use this as a starting point for their writing.

They will be told what type of writing will be tested, i.e. the type of text. This will either be a narrative, a persuasive text, a description, a procedure or an information report.

For some questions we have provided three levels of sample answers: high, average and low. These are a guide to what will be expected. They can be used to help students assess or improve their own writing by comparing the details of the supplied responses to their own. They can be found on pages 187, 194, 201–202, 209 and 216–217.

Students will be given space to plan their ideas for their writing. At this stage the plan could be only a few words, a picture or some simple phrases. This will help them to trigger ideas and prepare to write.

Students will also be given space in which to write their response. This will only be a few lines at first, increasing in length with each practice question.

Helping students

If students aren't sure how to write a particular type of text, one way to start is to ask them to talk about the topic and to state their views on the subject. Next you could show them how to plan their writing. Then they can start to write. It may not be easy for them at first.

Give plenty of praise and encouragement. Remember that Year 2 students are still quite young. Emphasise whatever is good and overlook any errors at first.

Space out the time between the writing tasks. Do not attempt one immediately after the other as this does not allow time for development.

Come back to these errors at a much later stage, perhaps a little before you start the next practice test.

On pages 221–226 we have provided a glossary of some useful words to help students in their writing. These include a range of verbs and adjectives.

Now it's time to turn our attention to the first type of text in the Writing Test: the persuasive text.

TIPS FOR WRITING A PERSUASIVE TEXT

What is a persuasive text?

A persuasive text is designed to convince. It can be a poster, an advertisement or a letter. The aim is to persuade the reader to change their mind or point of view and to win the support of the reader.

You will use your writing to convince other people to share your views, so for a persuasive text state one side of the issue only. Are you for or against? You then support this point of view with facts and examples. Don't list reasons for and reasons against.

What is the structure of a persuasive text?

Introduction

The first paragraph is the introduction. Make this a statement of your opinion.

It should be a short paragraph of one or two sentences which introduces the topic and your viewpoint. It should be a strong sentence which captures interest, e.g. *Hunting should not be allowed as a sport. We should not harm poor weak animals.*

Arguments

The paragraphs that follow are called the *arguments*. The word *argument* does not refer to a fight.

In this context an *argument* is a list of reasons for your opinion.

The arguments follow the introduction. Focus on your main points and elaborate on them.

Some points to remember:

- Express your point of view clearly. Back up each idea, opinion or argument with evidence.

- Use a new paragraph for each new point or idea. Include reasons, evidence and examples to support your opinion.

- Try to include at least three paragraphs with at least two sentences in each paragraph. Avoid using paragraphs with one sentence.

- State your arguments or ideas in order, one after the other. They should be logical, i.e. they should make sense. Start with the strongest argument.

- Use linking words. Linking words are sometimes called connectives. Connectives are words that are used to join ideas. They make the links between ideas flow more smoothly. Here are some examples: *firstly, secondly, thirdly, another reason, finally, because, next, then, when, after, so, however, even though* and *although*.

- Use strong modal verbs, e.g. *will, must, should, can, might, should, ought to, shall, could* and *would*.

- Use the present tense for ideas or arguments, e.g. *I believe that* … Use the past tense to give examples, e.g. *I have heard that* …

Conclusion

The conclusion is a strong ending statement that summarises all your key points, e.g. *In conclusion, it is clear that* …

The conclusion does not contain any new information or points. The conclusion should be one or two sentences in length.

Here is a Sample Writing question for a persuasive text.

Topic: Should children get pocket money?

Today you are going to write a persuasive text (also called an exposition). The idea for your writing is **Should children get pocket money?**

Remember to:

* think about your view on the topic
* include clear opening and concluding statements
* plan your writing, thinking about arguments for or against
* use paragraphs
* write in sentences
* check your spelling and punctuation
* write about five sentences in total.

Use the persuasive text planning sheet on the next page.

Here is a sample planning sheet for the sample persuasive writing question.

PERSUASIVE TEXT PLANNING SHEET

OPENING STATEMENT

What do you think about the issue? Are you for or against? (1–2 sentences)

I think kids don't need pocket money.

ARGUMENTS reasons that support your opinion

Reason 1 evidence/example	**Reason 2** evidence/example	**Reason 3** evidence/example
Firstly, they get given everything they need.	*Secondly, it isn't fair if some do and others don't.*	*Lastly, kids are too young to look after money.*

CONCLUSION repeat what you believe

Giving children pocket money is trouble.

We have provided three sample answers to the sample question. The first is a good answer, the second is an average answer and the third is a little poorer in quality.

A GOOD ANSWER

Children think that they should get pocket money, but most parents can't really deside what to do. I think kids don't need to get pocket money.

Firstly, children don't need pocket money because their parents allready give them whatever they need. Everything else is just extra stuff that kids really want, like an iPod. Most kids want things that they think they need but really don't. You can surive without an iPod can't you?

Next, some families can't aford to give their children pocket money, so its not fear if some kids get it and athers don't. Also, they shouldn't be paid for chores, they should be helping out anyway.

Finally, children are too young to be hold money. They might loose it or spend it on silly things.

In conclusion, I think that giving kids pocket money is just trouble.

AN AVERAGE ANSWER

I think kids don't need to get pocket money.

Kids allready get whatever they need like food drink cloths toys. Extra stuff is just stuff they don't need.

Next some familees too poor to give out pocket money.

Kids allways loos money and someone steels it.

Kids having pocket money is not right.

A POORER ANSWER

Kids don't need pocket money

They have everytin allredy and they wil loos it.

NO POCKET MONEY!

Please note: Spelling, punctuation and grammar errors have been included to replicate the likely responses of Year 2 children.

We hope that these samples of writing were helpful. Now it's time for you to start writing.

- In this part you will be writing a persuasive text.
- Write your answer on a separate sheet of paper.
- Use the top part of the sheet of paper or the planning sheet on the next page to organise your ideas.
- Do not take more than 40 minutes for this writing.
- When you have finished, hand your writing to your teacher, parents or another adult to mark it for you.

Topic: Would you like to be a prince or princess for a day?

Today you are going to write a persuasive text. The idea for your writing is **Would you like to be a prince or princess for a day?**

Remember to:

- think about your view on the topic
- include clear opening and concluding statements
- plan your writing, thinking about arguments for or against
- use paragraphs
- write in sentences
- check your spelling and punctuation
- write as much as you can
- finish in 40 minutes.

Use the persuasive text planning sheet on the next page to help you organise your writing.

Here is a planning sheet to help you write your persuasive text.

PERSUASIVE TEXT PLANNING SHEET

OPENING STATEMENT

What do you think about the issue? Are you for or against? (1–2 sentences)

I think …

ARGUMENTS reasons that support your opinion

Reason 1

evidence/example

Reason 2

evidence/example

Reason 3

evidence/example

CONCLUSION repeat what you believe

In conclusion …
I believe that …

Use this chart to evaluate your writing.

GUIDELINES FOR WRITING A PERSUASIVE TEXT	✓ or ✗
Have you clearly stated your opinion?	
Have you written the text in a planned order?	
Have you written convincingly?	
Have you given supporting reasons with examples?	
Have you used a new paragraph for each new point or idea?	
Have you included at least three paragraphs with at least two sentences in each paragraph?	
Have you included an ending statement to summarise all the key points?	
Have you used time connectives to link the text, e.g. *firstly, secondly, thirdly, lastly, finally, next, when, then, after, however* and *for this reason*?	
Have you used persuasive/convincing words, e.g. *always, never, must, maybe, probably, often, can, might, should, could* and *would*?	
Have you used thinking words, e.g. *I think* and *I feel*?	
Have you used the past/present/future tense consistently?	
Have you used pronouns correctly?	
Have you used correct sentence structure?	
Have you used verbs correctly, such as accurate tense and number, e.g. *he is* and *they are*?	
Have you used punctuation correctly, such as capital letters, full stops, exclamation marks and question marks?	
Have you checked the spelling?	

TIPS FOR WRITING A NARRATIVE TEXT

What is a narrative text?

The purpose of a narrative text is to tell a story or to entertain. There is normally an unexpected or unpredictable chain of events that will make the story interesting to read.

What is the structure of a narrative text?

A narrative is made up of the following:

- **Introduction/Orientation**—here the characters, setting and problem that arises is introduced
- **Complication**—this reveals in detail how the problem arises
- **Conclusion/Resolution**—this shows how the problem is solved.

Hints for writing a narrative text

- Make sure there is a clear beginning, middle and end.
- Use adjectives to describe people, places, settings and objects in the story.
- Choose words to express the feelings of the characters.
- Use a variety of time connectives to join ideas and link the story, such as *firstly*, *next* and *later*. Avoid using *then* repeatedly.
- Use the past tense to tell the story but the present tense for speech.
- Make sure each paragraph focuses on one main idea or point only.
- Write sentences of different lengths. A story made up entirely of short sentences can be boring.
- Add expression. Thinking and action words help the reader imagine what the characters are thinking or doing.
- Use dialogue between descriptions. Try to use speech marks to show dialogue, e.g. *Abby said, "I might put a magic spell on Jennifer."* This makes the story more interesting than if reported speech was used, e.g. *Abby said she might put a magic spell on Jennifer*.
- Make sure you start and end in an interesting way.

Here is a Sample Writing question for a narrative text.

Topic: An exciting day with Grandpa

Today you are going to write a narrative or story. The idea for your story is **An exciting day with Grandpa**. Talk about what you did and what happened on this exciting day.

Remember to:

- think about the characters
- make sure there is a problem to be solved
- plan your writing
- use paragraphs
- write in sentences
- check your spelling and punctuation.

Use the narrative text planning sheet on the next page.

Here is a sample planning sheet for the sample narrative writing question.

NARRATIVE TEXT PLANNING SHEET

WHERE?

Grandpa's house, backyard, beach

WHEN?

Tuesday

WHO? (characters)

Grandpa, Mum, Dad, Aunty Carol

WHAT? (problem/main events)

looking after me while Mum and Dad are at work

SOLUTION?

fish and chips for dinner
funny stories, silly things

It is not complete but it is a good start.

We have provided three sample answers to the sample question. The first is a good answer, the second is an average answer and the third is a little poorer in quality.

A GOOD ANSWER

An exciting day with Grandpa

Yesterday, which was Tuesday of corse, I went to Grandpa's house. He was looking after me wile mum and Dad were at work. I thoght it was going to be a boring day. Aunty Carol came over and tried to make me some lunch but it was disgusten. She always makes us wierd stuff. Next we played games outside in the backyard. After that we went for a walk to the beech and my legs got a bit tied because it was far away. We also got to fly our kites because it was pretty windy. Then we had delishous fish and chips for dinner. Grandpa is funny. He tells me funny stories and he does silly things and tells me not to tell Mum or we'll both get into trouble! Finally it was time for Mum and Dad to come and pick me up. I didn't want to go. I had a fantastic day with Grandpa! It was the best day ever!

AN AVERAGE ANSWER

An exciting day with Grandpa

Yesterday, I went to Grandpa's house to play. Aunty Carol came over too and she made me some lanch. Then we played outside. After we went for a walk. We flew our kites it was pretty windy. After we had yummy fish and chips for dinner. Finally Mum and Dad picked me up. Then we went home. It was a fun day!

A POORER ANSWER

Yestday I went to Grandpa's hose to have a fun day we had lush we playd outsid we went for a walk we flyd kites we had dina we had fun with grandpa we went home.

Please note: Spelling, punctuation and grammar errors have been included to replicate the likely responses of Year 2 children.

We hope that these samples of writing were helpful. Now it's time for you to start writing.

- **In this part you will write a narrative. The writing can be an imaginary story based on something that really happened or it can be a story you made up from scratch.**

- **Write your answer on a separate sheet of paper.**

- **Use the top part of the sheet of paper or the planning sheet on the next page to organise your ideas.**

- **Do not take more than 40 minutes for this writing.**

- **When you have finished, hand your writing to your teacher, parents or another adult to mark it for you.**

Topic: An adventure in a hot air balloon

Today you are going to write a narrative or story.

The idea for your story is **An adventure in a hot air balloon**. Imagine that you are flying in a hot air balloon.

Talk about what you saw, what you did and what happened on this adventure.

Try to write between three and five sentences.

Remember to:

- think about the characters
- make sure there is a problem to be solved
- plan your writing
- use paragraphs
- write in sentences
- check your spelling and punctuation.

Use the narrative text planning sheet on the next page to help you organise your writing.

Here is a planning sheet to help you write your narrative.

NARRATIVE TEXT PLANNING SHEET

WHERE?

WHEN?

WHO? (characters)

WHAT? (problem/main events)

SOLUTION?

MARKING CHECKLIST FOR NARRATIVE TEXT WRITING TEST

Use this chart to evaluate your writing.

GUIDELINES FOR WRITING A NARRATIVE TEXT	✓ or ✗
Have you written at least three sentences?	
Have you told the narrative clearly?	
Have you written the story in a planned order?	
Have you introduced characters and setting?	
Have you included a problem, complication or situation in the narrative?	
Have you written the narrative in an entertaining way?	
Have you shown how the issue is resolved?	
Have you used time connectives to link the story, e.g. *so*, *but*, *because*, *since*, *then*, *later*, *however*, *although*, *once*, *suddenly* and *meanwhile*?	
Have you used thinking words, e.g. *I think* and *I feel*?	
Have you used adjectives to describe people, places, settings or objects in the story?	
Have you chosen words to express the feelings of the characters?	
Have you used new paragraphs for each separate idea?	
Have you used the past/present/future tense consistently?	
Have you used pronouns correctly?	
Have you used correct sentence structure?	
Have you used verbs correctly, such as accurate tense and number, e.g. *he is* and *they are*?	
Have you used correct punctuation, such as capital letters, full stops, exclamation marks and question marks?	
Have you checked that the spelling is correct?	

TIPS FOR WRITING AN INFORMATION TEXT

What is an information text?

An information text (or report) presents information about a specific subject.

What is the structure of an information text?

An information text includes subheadings and organised facts about the topic.

Introduction

The first paragraph is the introduction. This is a simple statement that defines the group you will be writing about.

Description

This is the main body of the report. It describes the subject.

This section is organised into subheadings describing such things as appearance, behaviour, habitat, diet, life cycle, location, environment and history.

Use a new paragraph for each different subheading. There may also be room for you to draw a picture to help your description.

Conclusion

The conclusion is a summary of what you have written or final comment about the topic.

Some hints for writing information texts

Try to remember as much information as you can about the topic.

If the topic is an animal, it will be easier if you have read about where the animal lives and its way of life. If the topic is a city, try to recall where the city is located and any other interesting facts about it.

To make the information text interesting:

- use as many adjectives as possible to describe appearance
- include action verbs
- add technical words to add more detail to your writing, e.g. for an animal use terms like *marsupial* or *antennae*.

Here is a Sample Writing question for an information text.

Topic: An interesting animal

Today you are going to write an information text. The idea for your report is **An interesting animal**. Write about an animal that you know.

Remember to:

* use your planning sheet to prepare the information text
* include a clear heading to show what your topic is
* plan your writing, thinking about the categories
* use paragraphs
* write in sentences
* check your spelling and punctuation
* write about five sentences.

Use the information text planning sheet on the next page.

Here is a sample planning sheet for the sample information text writing question.

INFORMATION TEXT PLANNING SHEET

INTRODUCTION

definition or brief description of the object

Sharks are scary.

DESCRIPTION   the most important facts about the topic

What does it look like?	Where does it live?	How does it move around?
Sharks are grey-blue. Have fins No bones Have lots of teeth	Live in oceans, lakes, rivers	Swim very fast Can jump out of the water

What does it eat?	How does it act?	life cycle
They are carnivores.	Like to be alone	Babies are called pups. Lay eggs

CONCLUSION

summary or final comment

Sharks are dangerous animals.

We have provided three sample answers to the sample question. The first is a good answer, the second is an average answer and the third is a little poorer in quality.

A GOOD ANSWER

Sharks

Sharks are part of the fish family. They are the scariest animals in the sea.

Appearance

Sharks are grey blue with a white tip. They have gills like other fish but they don't have bones like other fish. Sharks have fins and a large tail with rugh skin to protect them from getting hurt. Sharks have lots of teeth. They have about 5 rows of teeth. Sharks can be up to 6 m long and weigh 2000 kg!

Habitat

Sharks live in ocens, beaches, rivers or lakes all over the world. Some sharks swim up some swim down in the ocean.

Movement

Sharks can only swim forwords, but they are very fast. Some sharks jump out of the water to get their food.

Diet

Sharks only eat meat. Many also eat fish, crabs, shellfish, hoomans and each other too. They don't choow but gulp their food.

Behaviour

Sharks like to swim alone. The baby sharks even are left alone to look after themself.

Life cycle

Baby sharks are called pups. Some sharks lay eggs. Other grow inside the mummy like humans do.

Sharks are dangerous but fasinating animals.

AN AVERAGE ANSWER

Sharks

Sharks are like fish. They are scary.

Sharks are grey and white. They have a large tail and fins. They have sharp teeth ans are very long.

They swim in oceans and beaches.

Sharks swim very quickly. They can jump up to chomp on their food.

They eat meat and seafood.

Sharks swim alone.

Sharks have babies called pups. Sharks lay eggs.

They are creepy.

A POORER ANSWER

Sharks

Sharks swim in the water.
fins and talls grey with wite
Hav lots of teeth are very farst
Eat fis crabs peepel
Have babbie eggs

Please note: Spelling, punctuation and grammar errors have been included to replicate the likely responses of Year 2 children.

We hope that these writing samples were helpful. Now it's time for you to start writing.

- In this part you will be writing an information report.
- Write your answer on a separate sheet of paper.
- Use the top part of the sheet of paper or the planning sheet on the next page to organise your ideas.
- Do not take more than 40 minutes for this writing.
- When you have finished, hand your writing to your teacher, parents or another adult to mark it for you.

Topic: An interesting city

Today you are going to write an information report. The idea for your report is **An interesting city**. Write about a city that you have visited or that you know.

Remember to:

- use your planning sheet to prepare the information text
- have a clear heading to show what your topic is
- plan your writing, thinking about the categories
- use paragraphs
- write in sentences
- check your spelling and punctuation
- write about seven sentences.

Use the information text planning sheet on the next page to help you organise your writing.

Here is a planning sheet to help you write your information text.

INFORMATION TEXT PLANNING SHEET

INTRODUCTION
the city and its attractions

DESCRIPTION the most important facts about the topic

Where is it located?	What is the environment/ climate like?	Who lives here?
What is their way of life like?	What has happened here in the past?	What is interesting about this place?

CONCLUSION
summary or final comment

Use this chart to evaluate your writing.

GUIDELINES FOR WRITING AN INFORMATION TEXT	✓ or ✗
Have you written seven or more sentences?	
Have you used a heading to show the topic of the writing?	
Have you stated the most important facts or ideas?	
Have you used subheadings to organise information?	
Have you included at least two sentences under each of the subheadings?	
Have you written in a planned order?	
Have you made a final statement in the conclusion?	
Have you arranged the words correctly in sentences?	
Have you used adjectives to provide a detailed report?	
Have you used adverbs and action verbs to provide detail?	
Have you used technical or topical words to describe, e.g. *herbivore*, *mammals*, *marsupials*?	
Have you used the past/present/future tense consistently?	
Have you used verbs correctly, such as accurate tense and number, e.g. *he is*, *they are*?	
Have you used pronouns correctly?	
Have you used correct punctuation, such as capital letters, full stops, exclamation marks and question marks?	
Have you checked the spelling?	

What is a description?

A description depicts, illustrates or tells the reader something.

The subject of the description could be a person, place or object.

A description is different from a narrative or an exposition. A description is like an information report. An information report describes a group of objects, like penguins.

A description talks about a particular object. If we use the example of a topic such as penguins, then a description might have the title *Ricco my toy penguin*.

What is the structure of a description?

Introduction

The first paragraph is the introduction. This is a simple sentence stating who, what, when or where you will be writing about.

Body

Here you will describe the characteristics of the object. Include details of physical characteristics, how it acts, qualities and important features.

Conclusion

There should be a final sentence or paragraph. This can include a personal response to the subject.

Hints for writing a description

- Use specific nouns, e.g. *doll's house, electric train.*
- Include as many adjectives as possible to help describe the object, e.g. *smooth pink plastic roof.*
- Use thinking, action or feeling verbs to describe behaviour and give us an idea of how the object acts.
- Use similes to describe behaviour, e.g. *as delicate as lace.*
- Think carefully about the words you use. Use lots of detail. The reader has possibly not seen your object, so you need to give them as detailed a description as possible. A variety of adjectives and adverbs will help provide the reader with more information.

Topic: Your favourite toy

Today you are going to write a description. The idea for your description is **Your favourite toy**. Think carefully about the object you are describing. Remember that the person reading your text might not have seen your toy, so you will need to use lots of describing words to help the reader get a good picture of what you are describing.

Remember to:

- think about how the toy feels and looks
- use lots of detail to describe your toy
- use paragraphs
- write in sentences
- check your spelling and punctuation
- write about nine or ten sentences.

Use the description planning sheet on the next page.

Here is a sample planning sheet for the sample description writing question.

DESCRIPTION PLANNING SHEET

INTRODUCTION
who / what / when / where

toy oven
birthday present
very big
great toy

DETAILS description of characteristics

for a person:
- what they look like
- what they do
- how they act
- what they like
- what makes them interesting

for an object:
- how it looks / sounds / feels / smells / tastes
- where it is found
- what it does
- how it is used
- what makes it interesting

big rectangle, stove top and rack
smooth pink and white plastic
lights up red
sizzles and bubbles
pretend to cook things

CONCLUDING STATEMENT
my thoughts or feelings about the person or object

just like a real oven

We have provided three sample answers to the sample question. The first is a good answer, the second is an average answer and the third is a little poorer in quality.

A GOOD ANSWER

My Toy Oven

My toy oven is an excelant toy. My aunty Helen bought it for me for my birthday. The oven is humungous, it is nearly as big as me. It is a massive rectangle with a stove top and a yellow rack on top to hang spoons and things. The rack has a clock on it and has coloured butterflies around it. The oven is made of smooth shiny white plastic and has pink sides. There are also clear plastic oven doors which open. The doors have pretty pink love heart handels. You can open up the doors and see what you are cooking. There is room to put food, plates or sauspans on the shelf in the oven.

Above the oven is the grey stove top. The stove top lights up as red as fire when you turn it on. It also sizzles and bubbles and sounds like you are really cooking a bubbly sause.

Next to the stove top is a little sink. The tap moves from left to right and makes real gurgly tap noises.

I like pretending to cook things like cake, chicken and vegtables. I spend lots of time cooking like my mum. It is just like a real oven.

AN AVERAGE ANSWER

My Toy Oven

My toy oven is pink, white and grey plastic and feels hard. It has green butterfly stickers on it. It has an oven with cute doors that open. The doors are big, the stove top is small. On top of the oven is the stove top. It has two round circles that look like eyes and they make sizzly noises. They turn red when you turn them on and light up like a real oven. It also has a sink with two buttons on it. The tap makes tap noises. You can pretent to cook things in it. I like my toy stove.

A POORER ANSWER

It is made from plastik
I like to cook on it and make cakes for my dolls
I can press the tap
It lites up

Please note: Spelling, punctuation and grammar errors have been included to replicate the likely responses of Year 2 children.

We hope that these three writing samples were helpful. Now it's time for you to start writing.

- **In this part you will write a description.**
- **Write your answer on a separate sheet of paper.**
- **Use the top part of the sheet of paper or the planning sheet on the next page for organising your ideas.**
- **Do not take more than 40 minutes for this writing.**
- **When you have finished, hand your writing to your teacher, parents or another adult to mark it for you.**
- **Try to write about nine or ten sentences.**

Topic: Your favourite person

Today you are going to write a description of **your favourite person**. Think carefully about the person you are describing. Remember that someone reading your text might not know your favourite person, so you will need to use lots of describing words to help the reader get a good picture of who you are describing. You can write about a family member, a friend, a neighbour or even your teacher.

Remember to:

- think about how the person looks and acts
- use lots of detail to describe your person
- use paragraphs
- write in sentences
- check your spelling and punctuation
- write about nine or ten sentences.

Use the description planning sheet on the next page to help you organise your writing.

Here is a planning sheet to help you write your description.

DESCRIPTION PLANNING SHEET

INTRODUCTION
who / what / when / where

DETAILS description of characteristics

for a person:
- what they look like
- what they do
- how they act
- what they like
- what makes them interesting

for an object:
- how it looks / sounds / feels / smells / tastes
- where it is found
- what it does
- how it is used
- what makes it interesting

CONCLUDING STATEMENT
my thoughts or feelings about the person or object

Use this chart to evaluate your writing.

GUIDELINES FOR WRITING A DESCRIPTION	✓ or ✗
Have you written nine or more sentences?	
Have you given a clear and accurate description of the person?	
Have you included an introduction or label, e.g. *My teacher Ms Erin*?	
Have you written in a logical sequence?	
Have you used new paragraphs for each separate idea?	
Have you varied sentence beginnings?	
Have you used similes for comparison?	
Have you used adjectives to provide a description of the person's appearance?	
Have you included a concluding statement?	
Have you used the past/present/future tense consistently?	
Have you used verbs correctly, such as accurate tense and number, e.g. *it is*, *they are*?	
Have you used nouns and verbs to give a more detailed description, e.g. *likes*, *protects*, *long red hair*?	
Have you used pronouns correctly?	
Have you used connectives to create compound sentences?	
Have you used correct punctuation, such as capital letters, full stops, exclamation marks and question marks?	
Have you checked the spelling?	

What is a procedure?

A procedure gives instructions on how to do something. It gives a series of steps to follow.

A procedure could be a recipe, directions, instructions for a craft activity, rules for a game or even a science experiment.

We are surrounded by procedures. Think about procedures that you might be familiar with.

Procedures use lots of commands and also steps.

Structure of a procedure

A procedure is normally made up of the following parts.

- **Aim or goal**—this tells us what will be done or made
- **Requirements**—a list of materials, ingredients, tools or equipment needed
- **Steps**—numbered tasks with optional diagrams listing in order what has to be done
- **Summary (optional)**—a short final sentence summing up or stating that the task is complete.

What should you include in a procedure?

- Commands in the imperative tense, e.g. *Put your foot ...,* instead of *I put my foot ...*
- Action verbs in the steps
- Prepositions that add details to the commands, e.g. *Put your foot on the pedal*
- Connectives for sequence
- Adjectives to give further detail about how the action should be done, e.g. *Carefully place ...*

Topic: How to prepare your favourite breakfast or snack

Today you are going to write a procedure showing **how to prepare your favourite breakfast or snack**.

Remember to:
- write the topic as a heading
- use numbered steps to show what has to be done
- use a diagram if necessary
- use action words and commands in your steps
- use adverbs to describe your actions
- write in sentences
- check your spelling and punctuation
- write about nine or ten sentences.

Use the procedure planning sheet on the next page.

Here is a sample planning sheet for the sample procedure writing question.

PROCEDURE PLANNING SHEET

AIM what we'll be making or doing

to make scrambled eggs

REQUIREMENTS what you need to make it, e.g. the ingredients, equipment, parts or supplies

eggs	*jug*
milk	*frypan*
butter	*whisk*
toast	*spoon*

STEPS in order, list what needs to be done and how you do it—if it helps, use pictures or diagrams to explain your steps

1. *Collect stuff*
2. *Break eggs in jug*
3. *Add milk and whisk*
4. *Heat butter in pan*
5. *Add eggs*
6. *Add salt and pepper*
7. *Mix the eggs*
8. *Stir some more*
9. *Turn off the heat*
10. *Put on your toast*

SUMMARY

Now you can make …
Now it is ready / complete / finished / done.

Now you can make scrambled eggs.

We have provided three sample answers to the sample question. The first is a good answer, the second is an average answer and the third is a little poorer in quality.

A GOOD ANSWER

Aim

To make my favourite breakfast—scrambled eggs.

What we need

2 eggs, a splash of milk, butter, toast, a jug, a frypan, a whisk, and a wooden spoon.

What to do

1. Firstly get together everything you need.
2. Next break two eggs in a jug.
3. Then you add a splash of milk to the eggs and whsck them really well until frothy.
4. Heat a tiny bit of butter in the frypan until melted (about a spoonful)
5. Turn the heat to low.
6. Carefully add the egg mixture.
7. Add salt and pepper if you like.
8. As soon as the eggs start to become hard mix around with a wooden spoon.
9. Lastly keep stirring until all the licqid is gone.
10. Turn off the heat and place the yummy eggs onto your hot toasted bread.

Now you can make my favourite breakfast. (serves 1 or 2)

Ps—get your sister to do the boring washing up!

AN AVERAGE ANSWER

How to make my favourite breakfast

What we need

eggs, milk, butter, toast

What to do

1. Break eggs in a jug.
2. Add milk to the eggs and mix well.
3. Heat butter until melted.
4. Poor in the eggs
5. Add salt and pepper if you like.
6. When eggs become hard mix with a spoon.
7. Keep stirring until done.
8. Place on toast.
9. Now it is finished. Enjoy!

A POORER ANSWER

How to mak scrambuld eggs?

Put eggs in a jug. with milk
melt butter
put in eggs
put salt pepa
stir
if it dusn't wobl you are finished
put on toast.

Please note: spelling, punctuation and grammar errors have been included to replicate the likely responses of Year 2 children.

We hope that these writing samples were helpful. Now it's time for you to start writing.

WRITING TEST 5: PROCEDURE

- In this part you will write a procedure.
- Write your answer on a separate sheet of paper.
- Use the top part of the sheet of paper or the planning sheet on the next page for organising your ideas.
- Do not take more than 40 minutes for this writing.
- When you have finished, hand your writing to your teacher, parents or another adult to mark it for you.
- Try to write about nine or ten sentences.

Topic: How to play your favourite game

Today you are going to write a procedure showing **how to play your favourite game**.

Remember to:
- write the topic as a heading
- use numbered steps to show what has to be done
- use a diagram if necessary
- use action words and commands in your steps
- use adverbs to describe your actions
- write in sentences
- check your spelling and punctuation
- write about nine or ten sentences.

Use the procedure planning sheet on the next page to help you organise your writing.

Here is a planning sheet to help you write your procedure.

PROCEDURE PLANNING SHEET

AIM what we'll be making or doing

REQUIREMENTS what you need to make it, e.g. the ingredients, equipment, parts or supplies

STEPS In order, list what needs to be done and how you do it. If it helps, use pictures or diagrams to explain your steps.

1.   6.

2.   7.

3.   8.

4.   9.

5.   10.

SUMMARY

Now you can make …
Now it is ready / complete / finished / done.

Use this chart to evaluate your writing.

GUIDELINES FOR WRITING A PROCEDURE	✓ or ✗
Have you written nine or more sentences?	
Have you used a heading to show the topic of the writing?	
Have you used diagrams to illustrate the text (where required)?	
Have you noted the basic steps of the procedure?	
Have you listed steps in the correct sequence using numbered points?	
Have you listed all ingredients/materials needed?	
Have you arranged the words correctly in sentences?	
Have you used commands (e.g. *hold*, *put*, *place* or *lift*) to note what has to be done and how?	
Have you used adverbs to give further details about the action?	
Have you used verbs correctly, with accurate tense and number, e.g. *stir the mixture*?	
Have you used pronouns correctly?	
Have you used correct punctuation?	
Have you checked the spelling?	

GLOSSARY OF USEFUL VERBS AND ADJECTIVES

ACTION VERBS

act	exit	kick	pounce	skip	switch
aim	explain	kneel	pray	slam	tackle
argue	fall	knock	press	slap	take
arrest	fear	launch	protect	slide	tap
barge	feed	lead	pull	smack	taste
bend	feel	lean	pump	smash	teach
bite	fight	leap	punch	smell	tear
block	fill	learn	push	snap	telephone
blow	find	lick	question	snatch	think
break	fix	light	quieten	sneak	throw
bump	flee	listen	race	sniff	tickle
burn	flick	look	raise	snuggle	tie
carry	fling	make	rattle	soak	tip
catch	flip	manage	reach	solve	toss
chase	float	march	read	spell	touch
chop	fly	mark	realise	spike	trap
clean	follow	mash	receive	spin	trip
climb	force	measure	relax	split	try
close	gain	meet	repair	spot	tumble
count	gather	mess	ride	spray	turn
crack	get	mimic	rip	spread	twist
crash	give	move	rise	spring	type
crawl	go	mumble	rock	sprint	understand
creep	grab	nail	run	spy	undo
crouch	greet	offer	rush	squeak	use
cry	grip	open	sail	stack	vanish
cut	grow	order	save	stamp	wait
dance	growl	organise	saw	stand	walk
dash	grunt	pack	scale	start	wander
deal	guide	paddle	scare	startle	wash
decide	hack	panic	scrape	steal	watch
deliver	hammer	parade	scrawl	steer	wave
describe	hang	park	scream	step	weigh
dig	head	pass	search	stick	whistle
discover	help	pat	sell	stomp	wiggle
dive	hide	pause	send	stop	work
do	hit	peel	set	strike	wriggle
drag	hold	persuade	shake	study	write
draw	hug	photograph	shape	stuff	yell
dress	ignore	pick	sharpen	stumble	zap
drink	improve	pin	shiver	surrender	zip
drop	increase	pinch	shock	swallow	zoom
drown	invent	plan	shout	swap	
dry	investigate	play	shove	sway	
dump	jam	plead	show	swerve	
enter	jar	point	shut	swim	
escape	jump	poke	sit	swing	

GLOSSARY OF USEFUL VERBS AND ADJECTIVES

ADJECTIVES

Adjectives tell us more about nouns. Interesting adjectives in your writing give us more information about people, places, things or animals. Think about the adjectives you use in your stories and try to avoid everyday adjectives like *nice, best, big, small, happy, sad, bad* and *good*.

Try to use these alternatives instead:

NICE: kind, polite, fine, lovely, caring, gentle, helpful

BEST: top, excellent, greatest, super, fantastic, terrific, fabulous, great, wonderful, marvellous, amazing, spectacular, incredible, brilliant

BIG: large, huge, enormous, gigantic, massive

SMALL: little, short, tiny, microscopic

HAPPY: pleased, glad, joyful, cheerful, cheery, thrilled, delighted

SAD: gloomy, miserable, disappointed, depressed, unhappy

BAD: awful, terrible, naughty, rotten, shocking, frightening, scary, horrible, disgusting, dreadful, upsetting

GOOD: decent, fine, well, magnificent, enjoyable, lovely, useful, safe

Adjectives can fall into the following categories:

COLOUR ADJECTIVES

red	grey	bold	hazy
yellow	black	bright	light
orange	white	colourful	pale
green	pink	dark	shiny
blue	brown	dull	sparkly
purple		glossy	spotty

SIZE ADJECTIVES

big	heavy	massive	small
empty	huge	miniature	tall
enormous	large	petite	thick
gigantic	little	short	tiny
great	long	skinny	wide

GLOSSARY OF USEFUL VERBS AND ADJECTIVES

SHAPE ADJECTIVES

arched	curled	low	sharp
bendy	curved	open	skinny
broad	deep	oval	solid
chubby	even	pointed	square
complete	flat	narrow	straight
crooked	high	round(ed)	wide

NUMBER ADJECTIVES

one, two, three, four, etc.	identical
first, second, third, etc.	single
double	twin

TIME/AGE ADJECTIVES

ancient	first	new	swift
annual	late	old	weekly
brief	long	original	yearly
early	mature	quick	young
elderly	modern	short	youthful
fast	monthly	slow	

SOUND ADJECTIVES

crashing	musical	roaring	speechless
deafening	noisy	screeching	squeaky
faint	piercing	shattering	thundering
hissing	purring	silent	whiny
loud	quiet	snappy	whispering

GLOSSARY OF USEFUL VERBS AND ADJECTIVES

TASTE/TOUCH ADJECTIVES

bitter	dusty	raw	sticky
boiling	filthy	refreshing	strong
broken	flaky	revolting	sweet
bumpy	fluffy	ripe	tasteless
chilly	fragrant	rotten	tasty
coarse	freezing	rough	tender
cold	fresh	rubbery	terrible
cool	frosty	salty	thirsty
crisp	greasy	scrumptious	thorny
crooked	hairy	slimy	uneven
crumbly	hot	slippery	warm
curly	icy	smooth	weak
damp	itchy	soft	wet
delicious	juicy	soggy	wooden
delightful	leathery	sour	woolly
disgusting	melted	spicy	wrinkly
dirty	nutty	spiky	yummy
dry	prickly	spongy	

WEATHER ADJECTIVES

boiling	foggy	hot	stormy
breezy	freezing	humid	sunny
burning	frosty	icy	sweltering
chilly	grey	rainy	warm
cold	gloomy	scorching	
cool	gusty	sizzling	

DISTANCE ADJECTIVES

apart	from	local	near
away	further	long	short
close	high	low	within
far	little	out	

GLOSSARY OF USEFUL VERBS AND ADJECTIVES

APPEARANCE ADJECTIVES

adorable	clean	hairy	perfect
attractive	dirty	handsome	plain
babyish	dry	horrible	shocking
bald	fancy	magnificent	sparkling
beautiful	fit	nasty	stunning
blonde	fuzzy	neat	stylish
chubby	glamorous	old-fashioned	ugly

PERSONALITY ADJECTIVES

adaptable	difficult	immature	polite
adventurous	energetic	interesting	proper
affectionate	enjoyable	jealous	quiet
angry	entertaining	keen	relaxed
annoyed/annoying	exciting	kind	reliable
boring	faithful	lazy	rude
brave	fearless	likeable	shy
calm	furious	lively	strong
caring	generous	lonely	talkative
charming	gentle	mature	tidy
chatty	greedy	mean	trusting
choosy	grouchy	neat	truthful
clever	helpful	odd	weak
determined	honest	peaceful	wise

ACTION ADJECTIVES

active	curious	hurried	sleepy
bouncy/bouncing	droopy	jittery	slouchy
bossy	drowsy	jumpy	slow
busy	energetic	lively	sneaky
cautious	faithful	quick	speedy
clumsy	fast	relaxed	sudden
creative	frightened	shaky	swaying

GLOSSARY OF USEFUL VERBS AND ADJECTIVES

FEELINGS ADJECTIVES

angry	gentle	nervous	thankful
anxious	grateful	nice	thoughtful
awkward	grumpy	panicky	thoughtless
brave	happy	pleased	trusty
calm	helpless	proud	uncaring
careless	itchy	pushy	unkind
clumsy	jealous	puzzled	upset
confused	jumpy	reliable	violent
cool	keen	relieved	wary
embarrassed	kind	sad	weak
faithful	lazy	scared/scary	wishful
fierce	lively	selfish	worried
frightened	loyal	silly	youthful
furious	mysterious	strong	zealous

Thinking verbs (feelings, ideas, thoughts and attitudes)

accept	dream	need	suggest
advise	expect	notice	support
approve	explain	plan	suppose
believe	feel	prefer	think
choose	forget	realise	understand
compare	imagine	recognise	value
concern	know	recommend	want
consider	like	select	wish
decide	make	solve	wonder

MODALITY

Modality is the range of words used to express different degrees of chance or likelihood. Modality can be expressed in a number of ways:

Verbs: *can, could, should, would, might, may, shall, ought to, must, will, it seems*

Adverbs: *perhaps, possibly, probably, sometimes, always, never, absolutely, definitely, certainly, often, maybe*

Adjectives: *possible, likely, unlikely*

ANSWERS TO NUMERACY TESTS

NUMERACY TEST 1
(pp. 19–22)

1. **The third piece is the longest.** Did you pick this easily?

2. **3 TENS 1 ONES.** There are 31 ✦ shapes.

3. **23 34 48 65 80**
These are the numbers from smallest to largest. Did you write them in the boxes?

4. **10.** The sum is: $3 + 7 = 10$.

5. **8:00.** It is eight o'clock.

6. **30 cents**

7. **$6 \times 5 = 30$**

8. **4.** There are 12 crayons and there are three for each child so $4 \times 3 = 12$.

9. The **yoghurt** is between the cheese and the butter.

10. **36** 37 **38** 39 40 **41** 42 43 **44** 45

NUMERACY TEST 2
(pp. 25–30)

1. **642**

2.

3. **20.** $13 + 3 + 4 = 20$.

4. **one-half**

5. **South Korea.** South Korea is on five points.

6. **in kilograms.** Kilograms are used to measure weight.

7.  This clock shows how it should look. The small hand should be halfway between the 3 and 4 (allow for some variation); the big hand should be on the six.

8. **$1.65.** The prices are 35c (pear), 95c (kiwi fruit) and 35c (banana). Added together these prices equal $1.65.

9. **60.** $36 + 24$ equals 60. Be careful when adding the six and four.

10. 😐

11. **14 cm.** This answer is closest to the length.

12.

Here is a chart to show you what happens when the shapes are flipped horizontally:

    Start

   Flip over to the side (horizontal)

13. **28.** These numbers are descending or decreasing by 2 at a time:
    38   36   34   32   30   then   28.
    Did you see the pattern?

14. **A.** This path is $5 + 12 - 2 = 15$. This was probably something new for you.

15. **less than 39.** It requires 33 moves.

NUMERACY TEST 3
(pp. 32–38)

1. **18.** You can count the number of billiard balls. Or, as there are 6 in each group and 3 groups altogether, you can multiply, so $3 \times 6 = 18$. Did you colour in the correct circle?

2. **4.** There are 4 people in our home. There were once 6 but 2 are now married. The other answers are unlikely. For instance, it is unlikely there are 0 people at our home (it is possible but unlikely) and unlikely that there are 14 (it is possible but unlikely) and very unlikely that there are as many as 24 or 40 (it is possible but very unlikely).

3.  The last picture is correct.

4. **9.** The complete sum is $18 \div 2 = 9$.

5. **36.** The sum is $12 \times 3 = 36$. Revise your basic multiplication facts if needed.

6. The shape that you would see is the outline:

7. **45 cm**

8. **8.** There are 24 sheep and there are 8 in each group ($3 \times 8 = 24$ or $24 \div 3 = 8$).

9. **430.** Be careful when counting up from 429. Remember that the thirties come after the twenties.

10. **21.** The complete sum is $30 - 21 = 9$.

11. **24, 15, 3.** The numbers are decreasing by three: 27, 24, 21, 18, 15, 12, 9, 6, 3, 0.

12.

This is our answer. You need to look closely as there are differences between the figures.

13. **30 minutes.** The digital clock shows 9 o'clock and the bedroom clock shows half past nine. The minute hand is on the six, so there are 30 minutes between the two times.

14. **The weight is more than 7 kg and less than 8 kg.** The weight is around $7\frac{1}{2}$ kg, which is in between 7 and 8.

15. **The first answer is correct.** The arrow is the only shape to have one line of symmetry. One way to check is when the shape is folded, both halves should fit on top of each other perfectly. The lines of symmetry of the other shapes are shown below.

16. **5 × 6.** There are 6 rows of 5 blocks. So the way to work out the answer is to multiply 5×6, which gives you a total of 30 blocks.

17. **10.** There are four quarters in one orange and two quarters in half an orange, so there are $4 + 4 + 2 = 10$ quarters altogether.

18. **D.** This is in the top row and is the third space from the right.

19. **$5.** The cost of the items is $7 plus $8 which is $15. Take $15 away from the $20 that Nicholas gave to the shop employee and this leaves $5 change.

20.

9	5	1
4	3	8
2	7	6

The answer is shown above for you. The trick is to look at one row at a time.

NUMERACY TEST 4
(pp. 40–50)

1. **The girl has more books.**

2. **28.** The girl has 16 books and the boy has 12 books. This makes 28 books altogether.

3. **one-quarter.** Remember that if you want to change your answer just erase it and colour in the circle you want.

4. **20c, 20c, 5c**. This gives you 45 cents.

5. **3 + 5 = 8.** There are 8 paintbrushes altogether. There are 3 in one group and 5 in the other.

6. **10:15 am**

7. **camel.** The camel is in the section marked A2.

8. **B3.** The well is in the section marked B3.

9. **South.** South is the opposite of North on a compass or a map.

10. **The Entrance.** This is the most northern town.

11. **North.** From Bateau Bay Village to The Entrance is North.

12. **9.** This is because $13 + 7 = 20$ and $11 + 9 = 20$.

13. **33.** This is a series of odd numbers.

14. **millilitres.** Medicine is likely to be given in small quantities and so would be measured in millilitres.

15. **A.** This chart shows you what happens when something is flipped vertically. The letter A does not look the same when flipped vertically.

A C D E   Original

∀ C D E   Turned over/ Flipped vertically

16. **15.** This is because you need 15 ten-cent coins (15×10 cents $= 150$ cents or $1.50).

17. There are **60 minutes** in an hour.

18. **$5.00.** If you add the amounts $3.10 and $1.90, the total is $5.00.

19. **115**

20. **15.** You have to do the multiplication first. So $2 \times 7 + 5 - 4 = ?$ becomes
$$14 + 5 - 4 = 19 - 4 = 15.$$

21. **There are more rowboats than canoes and yachts.** There are 12 rowboats, 8 canoes and 3 yachts. Do you understand how to read the chart?

22. **27 August.** Remember that Monday to Monday is a week. So it is one week to the 13th, two weeks to the 20th and 3 weeks to the 27th. This may have been a little tricky for you.

23. **1 out of 6 chances.** When we throw the dice it could land anywhere. There are six faces so the chance of a face being on top is called one in six. Sometimes it will be a four and sometimes it will not. Overall we expect that it will be the number that we want about one in every six times.

24. **8 dots.** You add the dots in the first two columns.

25. **50.** The answer to the sum $37 + 12$ is 49 and 50 is the closest number. To estimate the answer you would change the sum to $40 + 10 = 50$.

NUMERACY TEST 5
(pp. 52–62)

1. **triangle, rectangle.** Five triangles and one rectangle make up the basic shape.

2. **six (6) hundreds, three (3) tens and two (2) units.** You can write this in words or in numbers.

3. **11**

4. Start your line from this dot

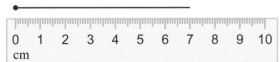

5. **508, 488.** 508 is 10 more than 498 and 488 is 10 less.

6.

7. **2.** There are 11 tyres. This means three tyres in each group plus two left over.

8. This is the net of a triangular prism. This is what it looks like:

9. **500 mL**

10. **20.** There are 12 lilies and 8 daisies $(12 + 8 = 20)$.

11. **South.** The university is in the North and so you have to travel South to get to the school.

12. **West.** Gardeners Road is to the west of Anzac Parade.

13. **5.** There are 30 flowers. You can make five bunches with six tulips in each—this is a total of 30 flowers $(5 \times 6 = 30)$.

14. The second answer is correct. We have tried to show this below (it is not drawn to scale). When you put both halves together you get a rectangular shape.

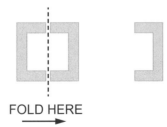

FOLD HERE

15. **11 cm.** The top rope is 15 cm long which is 11 more than the length of the other rope. It is $15 - 4 = 11$.

16. **$2.50.** Here you first have to multiply the cost of the toffee apple by two and then add the price of a candy bar ($1 \times 2 = 2 plus 50 cents $= 2.50).

17. **29.** The numbers decrease by 3. We start with 50 then subtract 3 to make 47. Then we subtract another 3 from 47 to make 44, and so on. Did you write your answer in the box?

18. Teve. This is the second lowest. Did you notice that the words 'second lowest' were in bold. This is to make sure that you do not miss them.

TOWN	RAINFALL (mL)
Dasher	200
Cuter	40
Pinter	35
Liulb	10
Teve	25

19.

This is the pattern of tiles that you should have used. There is one white, one grey, and two that are half-grey and half-white.

20. 8. This is shown in the diagram below:

21.  is how the image will appear from the inside of Lucky's window.

22. 195

23. Ann. She lived there for 11 years from 2000 to 2011.

24. Gail lived in the street longer than Dawn.

25. 6 years, Mark

26. multiply $1800 by 4

27. An even number is an odd number plus one.

28. Today is Friday. It is Friday because he plays tomorrow, and tomorrow is Saturday.

29. A 1 or a 6 are equally likely. When you throw a die it is certain the number will be from 1 to 6 but all numbers have the same chance.

30. one-third. Bunt asked for two pieces that were each one-third in size. If you double a third of a cake then you will have two-thirds and this is more than half a cake but less than a whole cake. This was a difficult question so do not worry if it was a little hard for you.

NUMERACY TEST 6
(pp. 65–77)

1. 43

2.

The second tree is the tallest tree.

3. 149

4. pyramid

5. The third figure is a set of scales. Weight or mass is measured using a scale. A clock shows the time, a ruler measures length and a thermometer is used to measure temperature.

6. $1, 50c, 20c, 5c. Added together their total value is $1.75.

7.

The third shape is a hexagon. A hexagon has six sides.

8. 32

9. 150 mL. There are 150 mL of milk in the baby bottle.

10. 8. There are 16 stars so if we gave half away we would be left with 8 stars.

11. 10:30. Half past ten looks like this in digital time: 10:30. Do you understand how to read digital and analog time?

12. 8 + 8 + 8 + 8

13. 35, 41

14. 14. The second Wednesday is the 14th day of the month.

15. The error is that there are only 30 days in April. This calendar shows 31.

16. **B3.** ◈ is at B3. To read a graph like this you need to start down the bottom of the graph with the letters, then with your finger follow the column across until you reach the symbol. Then move your finger up to see which number it matches.

17. **$25**

18. **6**

19. **60 ÷ 10**

20. **9.** This chart shows you where the diamonds fit into the larger shape.

21. ❖. The pattern is quite simple: objects are arranged in pairs. The four diamonds would have been the second in the pair. We hope that this was not too tricky for you.

22. **12.** 29 + 13 is the same as 30 + 12. Sometimes you will find these easy and sometimes the questions will be a little hard. Use some spare paper to work things out if you need to.

23. **22.** He serviced 22. Remember that ⦀⦀ is equal to 5.

24. **6.** Since four drinks fit in each carton, six cartons will be needed. Twenty (20) drinks fit into five cartons but then there are two left over which she will need to put in one more carton.

25. **8.** The pattern here is that the numbers are reducing by 6, so the next number would be 8.

26. **10.** An extra row is being added to each pattern: first two, then three and then four.

27. **between 12 and 18**

28.

The second answer is correct.

29. **$15 − $3.50 − $5 − $4**

30. **54.** The answer is 62 − 8 = 54.

31. **45 minutes.** The next bus to Leichhardt is at 10:15 and it is now 9:30, so the difference is 45 minutes.

32. **They multiply the left number by 5.**

33. **5 − 3 + 1 = 3**

34. **6 and 3.** This is not easy to work out but you can solve it by trying different answers to see which works best. You can check all the numbers that add up to 9 to see which one is double the other (1 and 8; 2 and 7; 3 and 6; 4 and 5).

35.

The third answer is correct.

36. **12.** At age 4 Rosie will have 6 spots; at age 5 she will have 7 spots; at age 6 she will have 8 spots, 9 spots at age 7, 10 spots at age 8, 11 at age 9 and 12 at age 10. The secret pattern is that we are adding one spot for each year after her first birthday. So each year she has 2 more spots than her age. This table will make things clear for you. This was a tricky question. Do not worry if it was too hard for you.

AGE	SECRET PATTERN	NUMBER OF SPOTS
1	3	3
2	3 + 1	4
3	3 + 2	5
4	3 + 3	6
5	3 + 4	7
6	3 + 5	8
7	3 + 6	9
8	3 + 7	10
9	3 + 8	11
10	3 + 9	12

READING TEST 1
(pp. 80–83)

1. **Happy.** *Happy* means that you have a good birthday.
2. **Summer holiday.** This should have been an easy question for you.
3. **blue**
4. **summer**
5. **to be on vacation**
6. **The last thing they want is to ever grow old.** They are enjoying this time of life. When you grow older there is more work and responsibility.
7. **frozen fish.** The frozen fish is $4.15.
8. **$29.80**
9. **689 Cazna Parade, Maroubra Junction.** Both the street and the suburb are needed in your answer.
10. **supermarket**

READING TEST 2
(pp. 85–90)

1. **five dollars**
2. **Australia**
3. **how a movie is made**
4. **Rain.** This is the name or title of the poem.
5. **Robert Louis Stevenson**
6. **sea.** This ends with the same sound as *tree*.
7. **on the umbrellas**
8. **You would find the poem in *A Child's Garden of Verses*.** This is a book of verses or poems for children. *The Black Arrow* is a story written by Robert Louis Stevenson.
9. **Michaela.** (Note to parents and teachers: this text is around grade 3 reading level.)
10. **The light from the sun is white.**
11. **the tiny parts of the air that we cannot see**
12. **blue**
13. **He was riding his bike home from school and was robbed.** (Note to parents and teachers: this text is around grade 2.8 reading level.)
14. **a young boy from another school**

15. **hospital.** We hoped that you liked this short story as it shows how we must always help people in need.

READING TEST 3
(pp. 92–98)

1. **It is a sign asking people to see children's art.**
2. **their sculptures**
3. **a show**
4. **Central Library**
5. **five.** (Note to parents and teachers: this text is around grade 4 reading level.)
6. **reading**
7. **plays soccer**
8. **She would like to play for the Australian women's soccer team.**
9. **through the town.** (Note to parents and teachers: this text is around grade 5 reading level, which is higher than it might seem at first sight.)
10. **a nightgown**
11. **the number of children reading library books**
12. **gown**
13. **ingredients and directions for cooking**
14. **Some things are too hot to touch.**
15. **tablespoon**
16. **half a cup**
17. **If you have plenty and you want even more you might lose everything.** (Note to parents and teachers: this text is around grade 1 reading level.)
18. **The Goose and the Golden Egg.** This is the actual title of the story.
19. **in a hurry**
20. **He thought that the goose had all the golden eggs inside her.**

READING TEST 4
(pp. 100–108)

1. **B**

2. **A**

3. **Funny-face sandwiches.** (Note to parents and teachers: this text is around grade 3 reading level.)

4. **Betty**

5. **She is trying to convince Joanne to make funny-face sandwiches.**

6. **A sandwich does not need to be boring.**

7. **a part**

8. **the man**

9. **no.** The man ended up fighting rather than talking.

10. **Hide-and-seek.** (Note to parents and teachers: this text is around grade 3 reading level.)

11. **It is a game that you play with other children.**

12. **They are safe if they run home without being touched.**

13. **the first person who is touched when they run home**

14. **Yes, it is possible to be 'in' if everyone else is safe.**

15. **1) Choose a spot and call it 'home'.**
    2) One person has to be 'in'. They close their eyes and count to 20.
    3) While the counter is counting, everyone runs away to hide.
    4) The counter shouts, 'Coming, ready or not!'
    5) The person 'in' spots other children and touches them before they make it home.
    6) The first caught is 'in' for the next game.

16. **The game is finished when the last person is touched or makes it home safe.**

17. The following answers are correct: **Koalas are brown and grey in colour; Koalas eat gum leaves; Koalas are furry animals.** (Note to parents and teachers: this text is around grade 3 reading level.)

18. The three correct answers are: **Koalas live in trees; Koalas are herbivores; Koalas are marsupials.**

19. **The coloured areas are shown.**

They should include Queensland, New South Wales, Victoria and South Australia.

20. *Gula* is an Aboriginal word for koala; **Koalas are furry; Koalas eat leaves; A baby koala stays in its mother's pouch.**

21. **He was honest.** (Note to parents and teachers: this text is around grades 3 to 4 reading level.)

22. **He wanted to help his family.**

23. **He did not give up easily.**

24. The story is about a boy who **helps his family.**

25. **fortune**

READING TEST 5
(pp. 110–119)

1. **Singapore.** (Note to parents and teachers: this text is grade 3 reading level.)

2. **small port**

3. **in apartments**

4. **He would like to go to Singapore again.**

5. **Temasek**

6. **the title page**

7. **Jonathan Swift**

8. **It is a book about someone's adventures.**

9. **something that is far away**

10. **They are both a trip that someone makes.**

11. **Sitting on the veranda.** This is the actual name of the text. (Note to parents and teachers: this text is grade 3 reading level.)

12. **no**

13. **been**

14. **the back veranda of a house.** This is the most important location for the story.

15. **porch.** This might have been a little hard for you.

16. **pelican**

17. **lilly pillies**

18. **the awning, the sunrise**

19.

20. **He likes the peace of the morning.**

21. **Emus are birds but they can't fly; Emus eat grass, seeds and insects.**

22.

23. **50 km per hour**

24. **incubate**

25. **This is a poem about the game we enjoy most of all.** (We have changed the words and meaning of the original poem.)

26. **winter**

27. **He saw a speck in the distance.** (Note to parents and teachers: this text is grade 3 reading level.)

28. **They were worried because it was unusual to see a stranger.**

29. **John came up with a solution to the problem.**

30. **This is a story about kindness to strangers.**

READING TEST 6
(pp. 122–135)

1.

2. **very fine leaves.** Pine leaves are like very fine green needles. (For teachers and parents: this text is grade 1 reading level.)

3. **It wanted to be a tree with leaves.**

4. **gold leaves**

5. **the fairy**

6. **They were blown by the wind.**

7. **needles**

8. **a happy ending**

9. **unlikely**

10. **Sometimes when we make changes, they can lead to bad results.**

11. **children and parents.** We think these are the main groups. The text is an old poster that is trying to encourage people to drink more milk.

12. **It is saying that milk makes you active and helps babies grow and be healthy.**

13. **energy.** This is another word for vitality.

14. **The order is 3, 1, 2.**

This is the correct order:

Frank The Lion © Copyright 1999

15. **They needed help opening the barrel.**

16. The boys were surprised because **Grandpa was hiding in the barrel.**

17. **Grandpa likes to play tricks.**

18. It is **unlikely** to be a true story.

19. The tone of the cartoon could be described as **amusing**.

20. **the stars.** (For teachers and parents: this text is grade 3 reading level.)

21. **A comet is a heavenly body.**

22. **path**

23. **Here is the completed diagram:**

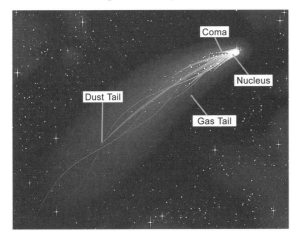

24. [blank oval]

25. **yes**

26. **poem.** (For teachers and parents: this text is grade 2 reading level.)

27. **She spoke with sadness.**

28. **humble**

29. **a miracle**

30. **Sometimes we do not really know everything about our friends.**

31. **R. A. Montgomery**

32. **There are many different endings to the story.** This is probably the best answer—some of the other answers are almost correct.

33. **King Solomon, the owl, John.** (For teachers and parents: this text is grade 2 reading level.)

34. **It was a trick to see who loved the bird.**

35. **injured**

36. **owl**

37. **white**

38. **honest or fair** (One answer is enough.)

39. **They were amazed** or **They were greatly amazed** (or something similar)**.**

CONVENTIONS OF LANGUAGE TEST 1 (pp. 138–141)

1.
    | Mister | **Mr** |
    | Road | **Rd** |
    | Street | **St** |
    | kilometre | **km** |

2. **.** (full stop). John played all his favourite games.

3. **!** (exclamation mark). Happy Birthday, John!

4. **?** (question mark). Why does the word "John" need a capital letter?

5. **sat**

6. **Joe and Jane catch the bus to school each day.**

7. **looks**

8. **us**

9. **we, her**

10. **Sophia rode the horse quite well.**

11. **The principal couldn't come to the meeting.**

12. **We liked reading Ronald Smith's books.**

13. **weather**

14. **extra**

15. **dress**

16. **collect**

17. **slight**

18. **stood**

19. **fixed**

20. **pay**

21. **goes**

22. **fast**

23. **beach**

24. **rocks**

25. **there**

CONVENTIONS OF LANGUAGE TEST 2 (pp. 143–147)

1. **was**

2. **or**

3. **die**

4. **will**

5. lived
6. was
7. go
8. of
9. can
10. make
11. My mother had an old mirror.
12. We placed it by the side of the barn.
13. Scarlett's ballet class is an hour long.
14. Dimi's house has two floors.
15. There was no answer. "How rude!" shouted Maddie.
16. army
17. pretty
18. would
19. could
20. week
21. twice
22. first
23. hour
24. seem
25. might
26. one
27. some
28. trumpet
29. hear
30. again

CONVENTIONS OF LANGUAGE TEST 3 (pp. 149–154)

1. like
2. on
3. is
4. then
5. high
6. are
7. their
8. for
9. and
10. by
11. sails

12. It's   weeks
13. town's
14. Police had to rescue families.
15. an adjective
16. I will be coming.
17. but
18. and
19. If
20. story
21. without
22. wife
23. head
24. open
25. short
26. round
27. become
28. reach
29. price
30. square
31. choose
32. Tonight
33. allow
34. frighten
35. black

CONVENTIONS OF LANGUAGE TEST 4 (pp. 157–161)

1. and
2. went
3. 85 Ocean Street
4. St Mary's High School
5. quicker
6. "You will need a bus pass."
7. His
8. Mary-Ellen, who is aged eight, is my new schoolfriend.
9. a verb
10. an adjective
11. a noun

12. I, it
13. so
14. compare
15. Lydia lost her tooth in class
16. It's important that you're ready before going to Mia's house to swim.
17. Nick is coming.
18. because
19. cost
20. class
21. care
22. move
23. behind
24. burn
25. clean
26. spell
27. poor
28. finish
29. hurt
30. around
31. learn
32. verse
33. together
34. large
35. straight
36. really
37. clapped
38. throat
39. thirsty
40. teacher

CONVENTIONS OF LANGUAGE TEST 5 (pp. 164–170)

1. They like the beach in Coogee.
2. an adjective
3. sit
4. caught
5. leapt
6. The big yellow bus was going into town.
7. The driver said, "Hurry along!"

8. George, Alex and Peter got on the bus.
9. We travelled to the beach on this bus.
10. After we got off the bus we had some lunch.
11. compare
12. My favourite car is a convertible.
13. compare
14. sitting
15. walked
16. eyes
17. rang
18. they
19. I tidied John's bedroom.
20. need
21. My mother and I swept the floor.
22. clear
23. maybe
24. across
25. tonight
26. tenth
27. see
28. these
29. those
30. full
31. eight
32. please
33. money
34. night
35. noises
36. surprise
37. further
38. siren
39. crowd
40. altogether or Altogether
41. careless
42. workers
43. unwell
44. kindly
45. smiled

CONVENTIONS OF LANGUAGE TEST 6 (pp. 173–179)

1. **Tiding** The surname needs a capital letter.
2. **fixes**
3. **Fred's**
4. **We** The beginning word in a sentence needs a capital letter.
5. **knows**
6. **takes**
7. **him**
8. **The Australian team played Italy in the final.**
9. **He comes home. He will rest.**
10. **I am happy to learn something new. It is always interesting.**
11. **"It is true that he will be on television," said Dad.**
12. **She said, "Excuse me. But is this the way to the art gallery?"**
13. **Use that path, which follows the shore, or go over the bridge.**
14. **better**
15. **are swimming**
16. **Peter's**
17. **, (comma)**
18. **youngest**
19. **I**
20. **of us**
21. **He and I**
22. **"Maroubra Junction School".**
23. **easy**
24. **its**
25. **are**
26. **live**
27. **light**
28. **cloud**
29. **space**
30. **queen**
31. **sew**
32. **coming**
33. **sign**
34. **easy**
35. **hopping**
36. **hotel**
37. **draw**
38. **window**
39. **mouth**
40. **goose**
41. **came**
42. **students**
43. **excursion**
44. **tough**
45. **heavy**
46. **large**
47. **gathered**
48. **canned**
49. **delicious**
50. **adventure**

To the teacher or parent

First read and say the word slowly and clearly. Then read the sentence with the word in it. Then repeat the word again.

Give the student time to write their answer. If the student is not sure, then ask them to guess. It is okay to skip a word if it is not known.

Spelling words for Conventions of Language Test 1

Word	Example
14. extra	We had an extra 15 minutes to play at lunch today.
15. dress	My new dress has gold spots on it.
16. collect	I will collect my lunch order from the canteen.
17. sight	Don't let him out of your sight.
18. stood	We stood up for a long time at assembly this morning.
19. fixed	Dad fixed my bicycle yesterday.
20. pay	I need to pay you for my book.
21. goes	Steve goes to soccer training every Wednesday.

Spelling words for Conventions of Language Test 2

Word	Example
16. army	Jason joined the army.
17. pretty	It's getting pretty late.
18. would	Would you like to come to my house to play?
19. could	Could you lend me a red pencil please?
20. week	Next week I am starting music lessons.
21. twice	I have been to Luna Park twice this year.
22. first	Tom asked if he could go first.
23. hour	It will take one hour to drive to Grandma's.
24. seem	You seem busy today.
25. might	I might see my cousins tomorrow.

Spelling words for Conventions of Language Test 3

Word	Example
20. story	Granny read a long story to Krystal last night.
21. without	Today I went to school without my jumper.
22. wife	I'm looking for a gift for my wife.
23. head	I bumped my head at gymnastics yesterday.
24. open	Can you open this jar for me please?
25. short	I went for a short walk before school.
26. round	The earth is round.
27. become	Evan will become a good soccer player one day.
28. reach	Dad can almost reach the ceiling.
29. price	What is the price of this hat?

Spelling words for Conventions of Language Test 4

Word	Example
19. cost	It cost a lot of money to fix the car.
20. class	There are eight girls in my class.
21. care	I will take care of that for you.
22. move	We will move into our new house next year.
23. behind	Mia left her water bottle behind.
24. burn	Be careful not to burn yourself.
25. clean	Remember to clean up your room before dinner.
26. spell	How do you spell your name?
27. poor	Poor Johnnie is feeling sick today.
28. finish	I will finish my maths homework tomorrow.
29. hurt	Alice hurt her leg.
30. around	Anna looked all around for her mother.

Spelling words for Conventions of Language Test 5

Word	Example
22. clear	The sky was clear this morning.
23. maybe	Maybe you can come to my house in the holidays.
24. across	My house is right across the street.
25. tonight	There are lots of stars in the sky tonight.
26. tenth	Lexi is the tenth child in line.
27. see	I'll see you later.
28. these	These pencils are very sharp.
29. those	Those shoes are Christopher's.
30. full	The glass is full to the top.
31. eight	We leave at eight o'clock in the morning for school.
32. please	Please close the door.
33. money	I have some money to spend at the canteen today.

Spelling words for Conventions of Language Test 6

Word	Example
26. live	Where do you live?
27. light	I want the light off while I sleep.
28. cloud	That cloud is shaped like a butterfly.
29. space	An astronaut goes into space.
30. queen	The queen wears a crown with jewels in it.
31. sew	I can sew a puppet together.
32. coming	Are you coming to my party on Sunday?
33. sign	The street sign is large and blue.
34. easy	My maths homework was very easy tonight.
35. hopping	I was hopping on one leg when I fell.
36. hotel	They arrived at the hotel.
37. draw	Ella taught me how to draw a unicorn.
38. window	Who left the window open?
39. mouth	Do not speak with your mouth full.
40. goose	The goose had a very long neck.

Notes